MANY CITIES

By the same Author

THE OLD ROAD
THE CRUISE OF THE "NONA"
THE JEWS
EUROPE AND THE FAITH
THE SERVILE STATE

Constable
London

THE CATHEDRAL, SARAGOSSA.

Frontispiece.

MANY CITIES

by

HILAIRE BELLOC

Illustrated by

EDMOND L. WARRE

LONDON
CONSTABLE & CO LTD
1928

Printed in Great Britain by
Robert MacLehose and Co. Ltd., at the
University Press, Glasgow

TO
MRS. FRANK COLLIN

CONTENTS

PART ONE: SPAIN

CHAPTER   PAGE

I. THE ENTRY INTO SPAIN - - 3

II. SARAGOSSA - - - - - 13

III. SEGOVIA - - - - - 23

IV. LARAICHE AND CADIZ - - - 31

V. TARRAGONA AND THE CATALANS - 40

VI. SALAMANCA - - - - 49

PART TWO: PORTUGAL

VII. VIZEU - - - - - 57

VIII. OPORTO - - - - - 62

PART THREE: THE RECOVERED COUNTRY

IX. ISLAM AND CHRISTENDOM - - 71

X. CEFALU - - - - - 80

XI. PALMA OF MAJORCA - - - 87

XII. SOUSSE, WHICH IS HADRUMETUM - 95

XIII. GUELMA - - - - - 104

XIV. CONSTANTINE - - - - 111

XV. CHERCHELL, WHICH IS CAESAREA - 118

XVI. TIMGAD AND VOLUBILIS: THE OUT-
POSTS OF THE DESERT - - 124

XVII. THE HILL OF CARTHAGE - - 131

vii

C O N T E N T S

PART FOUR : FRANCE

CHAPTER   PAGE

XVIII. THE MONUMENTS OF THE RHONE   139

XIX. ROCAMADOUR - - - - 145

XX. PÉRIGUEUX - - - - 150

XXI. THE GREAT HOUSE OF DURTAL - 156

XXII. CHALUS - - - - - 161

XXIII. VIRE - - - - - - 167

XXIV. LE MANS - - - - - 172

PART FIVE : THE RHINE MARCH

XXV. AIX-LA-CHAPELLE - - - 179

XXVI. METZ - - - - - - 186

XXVII. TREVES - - - - - 194

XXVIII. BONN - - - - - 201

XXIX. WORMS AND SPIRES - - - 208

XXX. THE VOSGES - - - - 213

PART SIX : TOURNAI

XXXI. TOURNAI AND THE FIELD OF
FONTENOY - - - - 223

PART SEVEN : THREE TOWNS OF LIFE
AND DEATH

XXXII. NARBONNE - - - - - 241

XXXIII. CHAISE DIEU - - - - 250

XXXIV. CORNETO OF THE TARQUINS - 256

ILLUSTRATIONS

The Cathedral, Saragossa - - *Frontispiece*

FACING PAGE

Cathedral and Roman Bridge, Salamanca - 50
Salamanca and the Guadarrama - - - 53
Casa da Concha, Salamanca - - - - 54
Vizeu, Portugal : Colonnade of Grao-Vasco
Museum - - - - - - 58
Vizeu : The Cloister between Cathedral and
Museum - - - - - - 60
View up the Douro. A Brunel Bridge and
Wellington's Ford beyond the Bend - 62
Fountain on the Ramped Pathway to the
Cathedral, Oporto - - - - - 64
The Bishops' Palace, Oporto - - - 66
The Tower of the Giralda, Seville - - - 76
The Tomb of the Alcazar, Seville - - - 78
The Rock and Town of Cefalu - - - 80
Cefalu : East End of the Cathedral - - 82
Cefalu : The Mosaic of the Apse - - - 84
The Port and Cathedral, Palma - - - 87
Palma of Majorca : Tower showing Islamic
Influence - - - - - - 88
The Walls of Sousse - - - - - 96
Sousse : The Rough Tower of the Minaret - 100
Kalaa Serhira, just North of Sousse : A
Roman Suburban Town, transformed and
turned Mohammedan - - - - 102
Guelma - - - - - - - 104
Guelma : Roman Theatre - - - - 106
Constantine : Mouth of the Rummel Gorge - 111
The Fonduk or Stable, with Mosque beyond
the Gorge - - - - - - 112
Constantine : The Native Quarter - - - 114

ix

FACING PAGE

Constantine : Corbelled and Tunnelled Road -   116
The Trees and Roman Harbour of Cherchell -   118
Cherchell :   Roman Theatre, Moorish Baths
   and Christian Church   -   -   -   -   120
Cherchell : The Aqueduct   -   -   -   -   120
Cherchell : The Single Column against the Sea   122
Avignon : The Bridge -   -   -   -   -   140
Avignon : Palais des Papes   -   -   -   -   142
Rocamadour   -   -   -   -   -   -   145
Rocamadour :   Roland's   Sword   and   St.
   Anthony's Chest (by tradition), on the
   Terraced Platform of the Shrine   -   -   146
Perigueux -   -   -   -   -   -   -   150
Perigueux : a Typical Feature on the Ascent to
   the Cathedral   -   -   -   -   -   152
The House of Durtal   -   -   -   -   -   156
The House of Durtal : A Courtyard above the
   Vaulted Cellars   -   -   -   -   -   158
Chalus   -   -   -   -   -   -   -   161
Chalus : The Outer Ward   -   -   -   -   163
Vire   -   -   -   -   -   -   -   -   167
Vire : The Tower Gate   -   -   -   -   168
Le Mans   -   -   -   -   -   -   -   172
Le Mans : The Cathedral   -   -   -   -   175
Aix-la-Chapelle :   The   Fish   Market   and
   Cathedral   -   -   -   -   -   -   179
Aix-la-Chapelle : The Shrine   -   -   -   180
Aix-la-Chapelle : The March Gate   -   -   182
Aix-la-Chapelle : The March Gate   -   -   183
Aix-la-Chapelle : Rathaus   -   -   -   -   184
Metz Cathedral   -   -   -   -   -   -   186
Metz : The Riverside and Cathedral   -   -   188
Metz : The German Gate   -   -   -   -   191
Metz : The German Gate   -   -   -   -   192

FACING PAGE

Treves : Porta Nigra - - - - - 196
Treves : Our Lady's Church - - - 199
Treves : A Rococo Doorway - - - 200
The Rhine at Bonn - - - - - 201
Rolandsbogen, above Bonn - - - - 202
Rhine : The Draconfels - - - - 204
Bonn : A Corner of the Double Cloister - 206
Worms : Old Houses on Market Place - - 208
Spires - - - - - - - - 210
Spires : The Cathedral through the Trees of
    the Close - - - - - - 212
Tournai - - - - - - - 224
Tournai Cathedral - - - - - 232

Part I
Spain

CHAPTER I

THE ENTRY INTO SPAIN

OF all the provinces of Christendom, Spain possesses most intensely that kind of unity and personality which come from a defined boundary. Things only are because they are one, and a city is most a city when it is sharply defined by a wall.

Now the Peninsula, although since the old imperial times so many accidents have come to divide it within, to make of its Western District a separate nation, to give Catalonia in the north-east a separate tradition, and to mark all the tableland and the Andalusian garden of the south with the scars of alien advance and retreat, has this geographical unity forever : it stands like a peninsular city cut off at its isthmus by a wall, a wall running from sea to sea ; and that wall is the very high even line of the Pyrenees. You have no choice but to come to Spain by sea or across that strict boundary of the hills— save at one doubtful exception, the Cerdagne. The note of your entry always, unless you come by one of those ports of hers which are so charged with memories, is the passing of a wall.

3

The roads by which you may so enter Spain are few. They may be compared to gates. There are the sea roads at either end, the high broad shelf of the Cerdagne, but in the main central part, more than a day's journey from either sea, there are three such passages only : Roncesvalles, the Somport—both Roman—and the new Sallent, which is close to, and not much more than a doubling of, the Somport. It is striking indeed to see upon the map, to experience with the senses in travel, the permanence of such a boundary in our time when half the energy of man is spent in multiplying communications. The great mountains run for twice the length of the Scotch border with no passage through for wheels. It is as though the Alps were thus shut over the whole line of Piedmont, with no St. Bernard, no Mont Cénis, no Mont Genèvre : as if the whole of the Swiss and Tyrolese frontier were blocked from the St. Bernard to Lake Garda.

I have entered Spain by many entries in the last twenty years : by Barcelona, coming from Africa and the Balearics ; by Cadiz, coming in a little coastwise boat from Laraiche, in Morocco ; by the Bay of Santander ; by Coruña and by Vigo. More often by the mountain roads—all of them—and again by the easy but high cols, such as the Bonaigo, which have no roads but tracks.

Whenever I so enter, whether by sea or by land, I find rising in me the same emotions as were provoked by my first glimpse of a new habit in houses and in men and of a new culture, unique in Europe, which came to me in that first voyage from Africa when I was young. But most strongly does one feel the contrast and change—the interest of exploration, the appetite for the discovery of new things, and the weight of the past—most strongly does one feel all those things when one passes into that proud, separate, and reserved world, not even by a path, nor by any entry commonly used, but alone, through some chance high notch of the ridge, where, not without difficulty but without peril, the mountains may be crossed and an approach made to Aragon through one of her innumerable parched valleys.

I remember one such entry, also many years ago—it was in 1907—when I had worked my way over a cleft on the skyline from which one could scramble down at last on to the Gallego.

There are many such opportunities—there are hundreds—in the curious formation of the Pyrenees ; and though they can only be used for a short part of the year, between the snow and the snow (when the snow has fallen one must keep to known tracks, and even then *deep* snow may render them impassable), yet they give to the traveller in these mountains an opportunity which he will find nowhere else in Europe : which is the opportunity for personal and lonely discovery. For though that wall is high and even as is no other of our mountain ranges, with very few regular passes, yet there are no glaciers—unless one counts a small attempt at one on the Maladetta. There are no vast fields of snow ; there are few precipitous formations so long that it is difficult to turn them. Indeed, it has been complained that these splendid hills give little sport to the climber. And that is as it should be—mountains were not made for the amusement but for the religion of man ; and to look to mountains for a game is like going to sea with a Bermuda rig.

At any rate, such are those hills, and such is the best entry into Spain ; to take, alone, any one of the many French valleys : to scramble up the steeps at the end, to pick one's way over the further side, going down where it may be just possible to go down without falling, and to make a passage of one's own in two days and a night from a road to a road, from a main stream upon the north to one of the Ebro rivers, muddy water rolling past burned banks under another and a more dangerous sun.

Such was that entry which I still so vividly remember, although it came long after I had enjoyed many others, by sea and by land.

6

I had left the last village and the end of a road which had grown vague and was at last no more than a few cobbles covered with grass. It had dwindled into a path following the little stream, until that path also was lost in the meadowland of the height, and there was nothing more to guide me but the thin tumble of water and the shape of the ridge upon the skyline beyond, 3000 feet above me. The evening fell, with a great moon, and the night made the sound of the water louder, as it always does. There was a little wind in the trees which hung upon either side of the vale. Before midnight it had died down, and I had then to come to the tarn which, in so many of these places, is the head of the water, with nothing but dry, steep rocks above it, up to the edge of the main ridge. These rocks, with the moon sailing beyond them to the south, were marble dark and looked not like what they were but like a precipice. I thought I would await daylight before I attempted them, and I lay down by the shore of the tarn to sleep.

The night was warm, even at that height, for it was early August, and the bare surfaces of these upland stones retain the heat of the day. I woke with the first dawn. Soon it was light enough to see what the task was before me— simple enough, but tedious. There was no track and nothing to indicate where, upon the

7

further side of the high circular ridge above me, I should find my best chance of getting down the Spanish side.   What I had to do was to make for the lowest point of that ridge, or what seemed to be the lowest point (for all was much the same height), toiling painfully up a very steep surface, now loose, now firm, and finding ways round occasional steeps of rock.   The business was long, though it was no very great height—no higher I dare say than the eastern face of Snowdon above its lake.   Before I had reached the summit the sun had risen, and as I set foot upon the narrow, topmost ridge, I saw its disc between the confused peaks to the east : and there, below me, lay Aragon.   The name alone is enough to fill a man with delight and to magnify him with the story of twelve hundred years.

It was up the torrent of Aragon that the swarm of the Mohammedans rode when they swept into Gaul.   It was down from that first beckoning of water that the first of the counter-attacks began, forcing its way down, march by march, generation by generation, till, a thousand years ago, the Christians held Jaca and Huesca a lifetime later ; Huesca, the town of St. Lawrence, the martyr ; the town from which, for good or for evil, we of Christendom got our institution of Parliament : King and Clergy, Lords and Commons, all complete.

That thunderous little torrent of Aragon

spread its name greatly outwards till Saragossa was taken; then the dark, awful range above the Castle of Job beyond; till, in battle after battle, after advances and retreats innumerable, alliance and counter-alliance between the Christian lords of rough keeps and the Moorish chiefs of the valleys, the tide came to an end on the heights of the sources of the Tagus, and the whole kingdom was formed.

More than Castille, more than Leon, does that advance of Aragon stand for me as the type of reconquest and as the beginning of those ceaseless adventures which are now the secret of the Spanish blood.

Once the Pyrenean foothills were left behind, the green, but burnt green, of their scanty trees and thin grasses was left behind as well, and the armoured men riding southward went over land in places so utterly bare that they recall the slopes of Aurès, where it stands above the Sahara, or those wastelands of the west, to which national pride alone prevents the Americans from applying the title of desert. The Reconquistadores went over a burning land; and this it was which lay now below me, far away, its glare not yet too violent under the early sun, as I stood upon the height of the main range, looking southward to where, so very far below, a deep trench marked the beginnings of the Gallego. Away to the west, beyond a barren high scar (which was red, sharply coloured, taking the full light from the east), lay that other deep trench, still in darkness, down which roared the torrent Aragon itself, the presiding spirit of all I saw, with that huge peak Garganta towering up into the light.

In the landscape below me and stretching so infinitely away (for between the shoulders of the foothills could just be caught the treeless plains) was the immensity of the past and the grave, profound appeal of Spain.

How often had I known that call! And yet, as I say, in that night and morning passage of the hills, I felt it more strongly than ever before. I was to see those villages which seemed part of the brown earth, and each of which has been called impertinently a museum, but should be called, reverently, a shrine. I was once more to stand astonished at the amazing pillars of sandstone as high as mountains which take the traveller aback as he turns the corner of the valley at Riglos. I was to come upon the first of the great churches which continue and grow to this day, and are the centres of this people, having in their plan, in the details of their ornament, in the uncompromising national seclusion of the Coro—like an inner mystery everywhere—the impress of something which is still of Europe and yet more individually itself than anything else of the West. For though it is a jest only that

Africa begins with the Pyrenees, it is true that
there begins with the Pyrenees a place sharply
different from ours, in some things older, in
others younger, having suffered crucifixion, having re-arisen, subjected to every vicissitude of
fortune and misfortune, of glory and of humilia-
tion, of satisfaction and regret; but, above all,
enduring and fed with an inward fire. Spain.

It is difficult to understand that degree of base-
ness and insufficiency into which men can fall,
men of the north, that degree of stupidity bred
from a vulgar pride which remains unaffected by
the sight of such things, by their memories, and
by conjecture on their future.

Ignorance plays a great part, perhaps, in such
folly, for ignorance will always take the tangent
to the curve; will think that what it superficially
touches for the moment is all there is to perceive,
and that from such a farthing basis the coming
fate of a people may be judged.

Indeed, this Spain, which I was now coming
into once more, is, to the full mind, much more a
provocative for musing upon future chances and
the perpetual eddy of change in history than it is
for brooding upon the known past—full of
tragedy, of splendour, and of burden as that past
may be.

No man coming into Spain but should think
long and deeply, not only upon the fall, but upon
the rise, of power; and especially upon the many

kinds of power and upon the vastness and complexity of those forces which move and intertwine like the eddies in the rush of the torrent Aragon, to weave and unweave, in spite of human will, the destinies of a nation.

CHAPTER II

SARAGOSSA

THEY say that no man touches the spirit of Spain unless he travels across its great wastes with the muleteers. But I should say that a Northerner will get that spirit more fully if he goes painfully afoot, communing with himself and marvelling at the endless barren solitudes around him. Or if he has not time or power to carry on through all those leagues and leagues and days and days of emptiness (on which the villages are strung out at great intervals like beads on a chain and the towns are half a week apart), then let him at least make trial of some interludes on foot, alternating them with the slow railway or with one of those innumerable motor-coaches which now cover all the roads in the north.

For here it must be said (as a digression) that no part of Europe has changed more in the matter of transport than Catalonia and Aragon between the Ebro and the Pyrenees. I find new and good roads where twenty years ago were mule tracks, and everywhere good and punctual petrol services, linking up the whole countryside in a network. This change is for the better. It does not concentrate men in one place ; it destroys nothing of the past ; it quickens the life of all these provinces.

Still I say, if you would get into the genius of the land, go as much on foot as you can, at the price of a very heavy tedium and (in summer) of fatigue under a new sun, worse than any you have known. For if you so act, you are under the conditions which those also were under who pushed back Islam : slowly recovered and rebuilt Christendom on these high plains, half-a-mile above the world.

But a man does well to travel in this way by winter as well as by summer, so that he may know the terrible cold under which the hardihood of the race has been tempered. The men who spread their language over the new world and (what was much more of a feat) their every social habit, their very cooking and slang ; the men who, for a century, held half Europe by arms and who at last wearied themselves out in the Dutch and German and French fighting, and in the attempt to hold at once all the seas, even in the north ; the men whose pignoned ramparts you find in Luxemburg as in Sicily, and whose exuberant stone carvings are in Arras as on the Pacific—these conquerors were tempered just as steel is tempered. For steel white hot is plunged into freezing water ; so they on these bleak roofs

14

of the peninsula, where the fierce summers turn suddenly into long months of clear and biting cold. The popular proverb has it thus : ' Nine months of ice and three of hell.'

The peninsula is a great arid, upland steppe, traversed by gaunt and barren ranges which run from east to west and divide it into broad bands : great vistas. With one straining of the eyes from the foothills of the Pyrenees (as from the Peña beyond Jaca) a man may see through that thin, piercing air, right away to the sombre lift of the Moncayo ; from the Moncayo (somewhat eastward) to the summits of the Guadarrama ; from these, to the high hills, sharp blue, beyond Toledo ; from these to the Morena, and from the Morena, I am told (I have not seen that last sight), to the snows of the Sierra Nevada itself, which overhang the southern shore. All Spain in four wide bands.

And this vast plateau falls down everywhere upon its edges to the sea, so that the whole land may be compared to a very high, ill-watered tableland of dust surrounded by a belt of low, luxurious gardens, stretched between the escarpment and the sea.

The masters of this people, those who have stamped their fierceness for ever upon the face of the world, and whose mark you meet, from California, eastward round to the Philippines again, were bred under the harsh, firm discipline of the upland wastes and ruled the fertile land below. It was in the bare high places that all the fighters of the Reconquista made their advance, thrusting forward from mountain range to mountain range, over the parched broad flats between. It is in the direction of this advance that Spain should be learned; from north to south.

Coming down from the Pyrenean boundary wall by the Gallego trench, you follow the main riding of the men who at last seized and destroyed the Emirate of Saragossa. You look upon things with their eyes, coming daily to things which are new to you, as such things were then new to them; leaving the trees and scant grasses of the foothills and coming to that incredible white wilderness, without a blade or leaf upon it, which, to the west of the Gallego, overhangs the Ebro. Indeed, even the man who travels by train down that valley gets some sharp impression of strangeness as he looks across the flat and sees mile after mile of leprous marl which looks not like something of nature, but like something dumped in a gigantic engineering feat, reminding one of those glaring heaps above the Cornish clay mines; but here the glare is a day's march long and hundreds of feet high, and dead and burned ash-white under the sun.

A man so proceeding also sees, what is characteristic of this land, the cornfields, painfully

recovered patch by patch amid so much barren-
ness. He has come from France, where, save in
the mountains, all is vineyard, pasture, plough,
orchard, or cool, damp woods, with watercourses
everywhere, and large, slow, clear rivers, humanis-
ing all. But he has passed a barrier like none
other in the world, and he is now in quite new
land, where a man ploughs what he can under a
vengeful sky—sometimes an open stretch of
fertile plain, but, for the most part, pockets and
exceptions in the stretch of dusty rock.

I have walked all day, on my way southward
to the Ebro, and seen not a score of habitations
nor one clear mile of tillage. It is not so, indeed,
along the river itself; but in the lands to the
west, if one has the curiosity to make that turn,
the traveller will see such savage loneliness as
he could not think to exist in Europe, not
even in the *causses* of the Tarn basin south of
Auvergne.

In such a landscape the works of man are the
more marvellous. You come towards evening
upon what seems to be but a brown lump of
the same earth, somewhat raised above the brown
dust of the way. You come nearer, and you see
that it is the grouping of a village. But nothing
tells you (till you are within the street) how much
the Mind of Man will here appear displayed and
triumphant. The church you discover to be of
the most solemn and most calculated darkness

within; all its woodwork carved with innumerable details, rich, fantastic, foisoning; its ancient windows calculated to subdue the light; its stones gloriously diverse with deep, personal ornament, and the whole coming from one national soul heavy with dignity and incapable of lapse. One could almost say that every large village had not only such a monument peculiar to itself, expressive of its inmost being, but also in the shields carven above the lintels, in the ironwork of the gates and balconies, in the house-balustrades of stone, a similar wealth of creative power. Such a village of Aragon is like an island in the sea, or an oasis. A special spot crammed with vigour and time.

Then, beyond again, the rock and the dust continue, and you look back in the mid-morning of your next day's journey, under the glaring sun, and all that hidden treasure is turned once more into a brown lump, hardly distinguishable from the burned stones of the plain.

The last long day's ride of the knights southward to the river, the last two long days of marching for the men afoot, took generations to recover. Christendom held Huesca while the shrill Mohammedan cry was still calling to prayer from the minarets of Saragossa. That Emirate stood out by cunning and by arms long after all to the south and to the east had fallen. But the King of Aragon at last rode in; and where the

chief mosque had been they began to build the
Seo, the central shrine, the greatest glory of the
city to-day.

Saragossa, of all the famous cities of Europe,
makes the least appeal to one coming by its main
approach. It had so much history and had
suffered so many famous things that already the
men beyond the Pyrenees a thousand years ago
thought of it as standing upon a high hill, conspicuous and fantastic. That is the vision of it
in the *Song of Roland*. But the real Saragossa is
nothing of the kind. This square mile, into
which there push back roots of two thousand
years, which still bears distorted the Imperial
Name (Cæsarea Augusta), which became the
capital of the proudest of the conquerors in the
full tide of the Christian advance and crusade,
and which in our modern time set an example of
heroism higher than that of any other city in its
furnace of resistance to Napoleon's generals,
gives no proof to the eye of its greatness.

You see, as you come in, the broad trench of
the Ebro, sometimes rolling a mass of muddy
water between its eaten, soft banks ; more often
trickling a parched, thin stream. Nothing is
conspicuous but the domes of Our Lady of the
Pillar, the very large church to the west of the
bridge ; on the cupolas of which Goya's frescoes
have cracked, in the very entrance to which is
that very ancient tradition of the West, the small

statue of The Pillar, older perhaps than Glaston-
bury. Save for those domes and for the high
tower of the cathedral to the left, there is nothing
to make you consider Saragossa as you take your
weary way in, parched and choked with Aragon.

But when you come within the cool of the
cathedral, then you perceive the externals, and,
if you are fortunate, you feel something of the
soul also which stood to arms for nine hundred
years until the great fatigue of the seventeenth
century came upon it and it fell half-asleep ; a
sleep in which it is now stirring.

It is wearisome to repeat the repetitive impression which these great churches of the Spaniard
leave ; yet each is of its own place and has its
own individual manner. Saragossa, less dark
than most, less awful, is more uplifted. And
this effect comes from a high lantern tower which
reveals with light the main altar and the north
end of the Coro.

When last I stood there it was the feast of
Corpus Christi, and there was some gathering of
people—not very many. The music was of that
strange sort with which Spain had long rendered
me familiar. Still more familiar were the words
of the ritual : all of these were what I had seen
and heard, I know not how often, up and down
the provinces of this land.

But what was peculiar to the heart of the realm
was the light coming down from above, from

the height of the tower. On the inner walls of it the laſt of the Middle Ages had nobly placed in woven carving the arms, the names, the titles, the dates of the building : a memorial : the bishops and the kings of Aragon.

It was not yet noon. The heat outside was an oven already ; but I was here within, sheltered, and permitted a recollection.

And it seemed to me, while I sat there so musing, that there is a double ſtrength in tradition. Firſt, the ſtrength which we all know, the ſtrength of continued names and forms which, though they become archaic and grotesque, bind the sons to the fathers, and are, therefore, most religiously to be preserved. But the second, ſtranger and more powerful, more full of body, is that ſtrength in tradition which has a resurrection about it assuring a continuance of life.

There is a sort of tradition which is not a form, nor a ritual, nor a name, but a surviving influence ; and this (said I to myself) is the abiding ſtrength, promise, and earneſt of the future of Spain. The vital memory ; the things *quæ olim promisisti ad Abraham et patres nostros.* To have such things within one, that indeed is to be alive.

So I mused in the cathedral of Saragossa the laſt time I was there. As it seems to me the paſt develops, continuous, and is alive in Spain ; like a seed still promising good things, whereas in so much of the Weſt the seeds have perished.

I can pay no attention at all to those who regard the cherishing of the past as an arresting, or a cramping; a check. Upon the contrary, it seems to me the privilege of a lively mind. For you may notice among men of middle age how most of them have grown intent upon the anxieties of the moment, or the base appetites of the moment, and have so become degraded with the passage of time. But here and there one man remembers not only his boyhood but his youth; not only his youth but his manhood, and is continuous with all he ever was. Such is the privilege of the Spaniards among the men of other nations. Such reserves have they for their next advance and for their rehabilitation.

A LL Europe is hungry for kingship : for the restoration of responsible power : for the recovery of a government which can not be bribed and which is stronger than secret finance on the one hand and its ally, demagogy, on the other.

Now there is in Spain one town where, above all others, this spirit of kingship remains as a sort of inhabiting soul, always alive, built into the very stones of the place and haunting the mind of one who dwells in it and surveys the past and the future. That town is Segovia.

Madrid, hard by, only one long day's ride away over the mountains, has been the capital for centuries. All around, at the Granja and in the sombre glory of the Escurial, you might say that kingship had far more powerful memorials ; while further beyond, above the trench of the Tagus, in the very centre of Spain, the hill of Toledo carries the ancient root of authority and was the central support of all this people for generation upon generation : Roman, Christian, Monarchical. And in Leon town are older origins of kingship, and even in the hills of Cavadonga or in Saragossa, of which I have spoken, or in that laſt ancient rough cloister of Jaca, where the firſt chieftains gathered under one lord, or at Huesca of Aragon a man might be expeċted to feel the thing more ſtrongly. But I feel it moſt when I see from nearby, peering above the duſt of the parched and rolling plain, the high belfry of Segovia. Then I know that I am coming, not only to the memory of kingship, but to the promise of its resurreċtion.

For Segovia muſt be seen thus, by a man coming in on foot from the north-weſt, if its charaċter is to be fully seized. It ſtands on a great isolated island of rock, which it crowns, and the lines of which it gathers up into the lines of its cathedral and great soaring tower. But it does not dominate the treeless, waterless, grassless, brown plateau of Caſtille. Though it is itself 3000 feet above the sea, yet is it somewhat lower than the immense empty billows of land to the north and weſt of it, and the citadel lifts up out of a hollow, dominating its own narrow, sunken valley, but not rising above the high plains beyond.

You come upon Segovia suddenly enough, if you approach thus and see, all in one view, the town close at hand ; not quite upon a level with the edge of the ſteppe which you have so long been tramping across alone.

It is an astonishing vision. There thrusts out towards you, compared by a hundred tongues and pens to the prow of a ship, the graceful strength of the palace and fortress, the Alcazar, which was the very heart of the kingship of Castille. To the left, the line of wall runs away along the edge of the rock, the town huddled within upon the uneven summit, and, at its highest point, the splendid mass of the cathedral. The two torrents of the two ravines which bound that rock meet just below the stronghold of the Alcazar, which overhangs them—the Eresma to the north, to the south the well-named Clamores : a torrent which, when the snows of the Guadarrama are melting, fills all the gorge with its noise. It is wise not to descend at once into the hollow, nor to approach the town by the nearer gate facing one from this west side, but to go round painfully towards the south of the city, where the bare land lifts upwards to the first distant slopes of the mountains, and to contemplate from that point the packed mass of the city, built of rock on its rock foundation. There the abrupt island of granite is united with the high land to the east by the finest Roman aqueduct in Europe, which they say that Trajan made. It still brings the clear water of the Rio Frio—the cold stream— from the mountains into the town. The Mohammedans left it to ruin, as they left everything, they who destroyed the forests and left such permanent scars on all the countries of the Mediterranean ; but at the end of the Middle Ages it was restored, and stands now complete, an immense series of arches, three stages high, huge blocks laid without mortar. The only thing I have seen to which it may be compared is the Pont du Gard.

Not this stamp and seal of Rome, which was built to stand for ever ; nor the cathedral, which was the last movement of the Gothic before the Renaissance, the last expression of the Middle Ages—but the Alcazar holds the soul of Segovia ; and *there* is kingship. While Aragon to the east was pushing back Islam and thrusting at the outpost of Saragossa, Castille swept in great rides over the burned upland, finding in the Guadarrama a sort of barrier which it could not finally force for many years. Halted on the hither side of that barrier, Castille dug itself in at Segovia, and that advanced post was the fortress of its kings. The walls of Segovia when Alphonso VI. rebuilt them (in the generation which saw Hastings and which was full of a tide of movement in Christendom already quick with the Crusades) were the crown of Castille.

It is again typical of monarchy, its perils and resurrections, that the Alcazar has been destroyed again and again.

At the time of year in which I am writing, in the heat of August, in the mid-thirteenth century, when the kings of Castille had had their establishment here for more than two hundred years, Alphonso the Wise sat in his great hall, with his nobles and his bishops about him, and, musing, said aloud, ' Had the Creator but consulted me, the world would have been made better.' Whereupon it grew dark and a flash of lightning fell and struck the Alcazar and destroyed half of it with flames.

That was but the first destruction. Others have followed throughout the centuries. The last was in memory of men now living, and it is symbolic of the spirit of monarchy that even in its last resurrection, even in our own degraded time, the majesty and dignity of that building have re-arisen. Indeed, Spain can boast what no other European country can boast to-day, that its modern building is continuous with that of its fathers. Therefore, the Alcazar, though nearly all the stones are new, and though only the great façade remains of the original palace, is still the shrine of monarchy. It is still the place where the populace rose, under the minority of Alphonso XI. (a little after Bannockburn), and where, five years later, when the child had become a man, such awful vengeance was taken against the rebels. It is still the place where, young and great, Isabella, the last heiress of Castille, was proclaimed queen : she who by her marriage with Aragon was at last to unite all Spain and to open the great century in which Spain made the

27

New World. It is still the same place from which that young, proud woman, only two years after her crowning, rode out alone and dominated the mob with her single presence. It is still the place where (again, how symbolic of the Crown!) he who was to be Charles I. of England, in that Spanish adventure which failed, Charles, the last to be possessed in his own country of full kingship, sat at meat and looked out of the high windows upon the tumbling of the Clamores far below.

Segovia was, and remains, the last of those intensely national kingly centres of the Reconquista, whence the final charge was made which swept all Spain into the Christian net; leaving only Andalusia to Mahomet as a vassal remnant. For it was hence, as from a base, that Alphonso VI. went out to seize Toledo, and to ride south as far as the Morena, and to plant the seed which three lifetimes later flowered in the final victory of Navas.

All this is in Segovia, and Segovia, as I have said, is kingship. Any one who would get into himself the spirit of kingship and revive the mood of that institution which was a necessity to our fathers, will do well to pass a lonely week in Segovia, thinking upon all these things. For Spain is now beginning the restoration of the kings. That with which Italy first startled the world not many years ago Spain has now undertaken : the re-erection of Monarchy. We are watching, with very little news of it and allowed very little comprehension of it here in the north, the most significant and the most profound of experiments. If the example shall spread to France, the victory will be won : the professional politician and his financial masters will pass from Europe and a moral anarchy will have ended.

Indeed, the new Spanish experiment is much fuller of meaning than Europe of the north and west has as yet grasped. In one form or another one nation after another falls back, from sheer necessity of living, upon this old stable model of personal rule, of real and responsible authority ; popular, not yet traditional, but already welcomed. Elsewhere than in Spain it is either masked by an electoral process, as in the United States ; or it is a dictatorship, as in Italy, with no provision as yet for its own continuance ; or it is a military organisation, as in Germany to-day— an act of police not fully developed there yet and certainly not yet fixed. But in Spain the riddance of the professional politician, the establishment of responsible and real authority is avowedly and openly a preliminary to the full establishment of monarchy: traditional, hereditary, popular, permanent.

Whether this good thing will succeed or no, none can prophesy. The chances are in its favour so far as public support is concerned ; one can be very sure of that, for there is not a nation in Europe but is disgusted with the falsehood, hypocrisy, and weakness of parliamentary oligarchy and the sham catch-words of 'suffrage' and 'deputy' which confused the nineteenth century. But two great perils, among many lesser ones, threaten the final success of the experiment. One is what was the running sore, and is still the scar, of Morocco. The other is the problem of Catalonia.

It is not for a foreigner to judge either of these; but it is for all observers interested in this critical experiment to note them and to watch their effect. For the rest, the main forces are in kingship's favour. The blood is there. The dictatorship is courageous, among people who worship courage; it is devoid of hypocrisy, among a people contemptuous of hypocrisy; and when the time shall come for the full restoration of monarchical power, there is a monarch present who can use it. Would that other nations to-day, after so long an atrophy of kingship, could say that!

Perhaps when I am an old man I shall return and stop again in my little inn at Segovia, and hear of some kingly act done, some kingly order given to a new Spain from the Alcazar of Segovia. I hope so; for the place should bring luck: and that one hardly feels of Madrid.

CHAPTER IV

LARAICHE AND CADIZ

THERE are one or two physical factors in the making up of Europe and Barbary which have quite definitely and clearly moulded history : we can talk of them as real factors in the story of our civilisation, not after the fashion of the popular modern guess-work, but with certitude. For instance, there is the wide area of marsh to which the town of Pinsk gives its name, and which, more than anything else except the human factor of the Mongol invasion, has separated the Russian from the Western culture. Here, in the South, is the Riff.

To the south of Spain, beyond the sea, over against the Andalusian coasts, stands the Riff ; such a tangle of mountains, such difficult ground for fighting over, as is not to be found anywhere else in North Africa or upon our continent. It extends in a forbidding, impossible band, cutting off the interior of Morocco from the Mediterranean, inhabited from the beginning by tribes unsubdued. The Roman organisation which was able to hold all the tangle of the Eastern Alps and the labyrinth of Albania, failed, or rather did not attempt, the control of that belt. No one has ever held the Riff, not even the Sultan seated in Marrakesh ; or in Fez close at hand.

To the south of it runs that easy trench by which the fertile Barbary of the east—Algiers and Tunis—communicates with the fertile Barbary of the west, of the Atlantic coast ; it is the trench Oudja—Taza—Fez, which has always been the road from the Mediterranean to the ocean, and which to-day the French have linked up again with a railway and with a wide military road.

As you go along this famous highway (which was also that of the first Mohammedan cavalry when they came in to destroy the relics of Rome), you have on either side great lifting mountains and the broad depression which forms a natural channel for traffic in between. The mountains to your left, to the south, are the first ramparts of the Atlas. Those to the north are the first foot-hills of the Riff. It has been the fate of modern Spain that this worst of all territories has fallen within her zone of government in the partition of Morocco, and therein lies the truth of that expression I have used, the ' running sore ' of Morocco ; that is, what long seemed the per-petual, and apparently fruitless, drain of the ceaseless Moroccan war.

No other country in Europe lay under a handi-cap of this kind ; nor will the foreign observer understand the first elements of it if he thinks this war a piece of purposeless aggression, a painting of the map. There was nothing of that in the debated and anxious Moroccan policy of Spain. If the Riff could be left alone (as it has been British policy to leave alone, as a rule, the tangle of Afghan mountains), the Moroccan problem would not exist. But there stand upon the Mediterranean coast, below those mountains, the very ancient Spanish towns of Ceuta and Melilla. They are not only an integral part of Spain and of her civilisation, they are of standing and importance in themselves. For Ceuta there was perhaps little direct peril ; for Melilla more. But all that coast was involved, and Tetuan as well.

They are not only of importance in themselves, they are also of importance to the whole European position in Barbary ; and their neighbourhood is always open to peril as things stand to-day. That is the heart of the Moroccan problem.

There is much else, of course ; there is the tradition of twelve hundred years, all one conflict between the Spanish people and Moors. The modern reader smiles when he hears that the keys of Seville and of Toledo and of Cordova are still treasured in certain Moroccan houses, but the thing is a symbol ; nor is it without significance that the Tower of Hassan outside Rabat answers to the Giralda of Seville in pattern, in character, in spirit. There is further that element which enters into all such problems : the difficulty of retirement ; the sound principle applicable not to all, but to nearly all, national tasks—that to abandon them would prove a worse evil than to continue the strain of them. There are these and many other considerations ; but the chief one still remains what I have said : a defensive problem connected with the ancient Spanish towns of that coast.

If proof were needed that Spain had here a task of quite especial difficulty, it would be afforded by the content and prosperity of all that part of her zone which lies in the plain westward, beyond the mountains : that open country through which runs the communication from Tangier to the interior : which will also carry the main road and the railway from north to south whenever, or if ever, the conflict of interests which meet at the Straits is resolved.

In this sea-plain, where also one of the last great battles between the Christians and the Mohammedans was fought out at the end of the Middle Ages (to the disaster of the Crown of Portugal), all now goes well ; and you will not find along that coast any more well-appointed, cleanly little town than Laraiche, its port. As a port it is hampered by a very shallow bar, the mouth of the River Kus ; but its good government shows itself in its external aspect, which is everywhere orderly. A man coming into

Morocco by this entry might well wonder why the occupation had become a by-word for anxiety and strain, for here all is at peace and all is flourishing. It seems also to have a natural bond with the coast of Cadiz, which lies opposite, at a distance comparable to the crossings of the English Channel, a matter of some hundred miles, most of which is coastwise running.

It was from this little port that I sailed over to Cadiz, which hitherto I had not known. It was a long, slow passage over the enormous Atlantic rollers, the last effects of a strong on-shore gale which had died down the day before. We crossed the bar with the afternoon high tide, and, after anchoring outside for a little while, the vessel steered north, and, as darkness fell, one could see, long spaces apart, the rare lights of habitation upon the African shore.

Our course took us gradually further and further from that coast on a line slowly diverging, but as we came abreast of the Straits, the great light on Spartel, the corner headland of Africa, shone brightly, and even seemed close at hand through the clear air. We caught soon afterwards the flash of the lighthouse at Trafalgar, and, with the last of a short night, we slipped in through the tortuous passage of the outer roads by which one turns round eastward into the sheltered Bay of Cadiz.

I know not what the roots may be of that strong

emotion which a man feels when he knows that he is touching the actual soil, seeing the very earth, on which very ancient things have been done. It is, in my experience at least, a combined emotion of travel and of history separate from all others ; a particular and special affection.

As we threaded into Cadiz Haven between the coloured lights of the channel buoys, I felt this strong emotion more than I have felt it before anywhere ; it was heightened, I suppose, by the night and the long vigil, and that first turn of the dawn which changes all things. Thus did I come in to the inner shelter of Cadiz, and they let go the anchor, and the ship swung to the slight flood tide. That same tide did the first inquirers from the inland tideless sea come to study curiously in the days when the outer ocean had no further shore and was a sort of eternity surrounding this world.

This place where I lay was the first of all the outer ports of the West to be known and used by civilised men. And throughout certainly three thousand years, and as much longer as you will, it has kept its name and even its form. Its name, which, they say (it is but a guess), may have meant something in the Phœnician tongue like a ' stronghold,' has come down unchanged in Latin, Spanish, and Arabic, through all these generations. The form of Cadiz has not changed either, because, by a happy accident, Cadiz cannot grow.

It wholly fills that almost insular site at the end of the long, exceedingly narrow spit of land which forms the natural breakwater of the harbour. Its walls, so often ruined, stand where they stood when Hercules first traced them, and the land gate is, and must always be, on one unchanging site. Cadiz is always of its nature a city on an island, and also a city more entirely of the sea in its traditions and changing fates than any other—more even than Venice. Though it was the last refuge of national government in the resistance to Napoleon it never attempted to govern the mainland. It has ever lived wholly by its harbour. Its alternate wealth and decline have gone with nothing but the alternate growth and lessening of its ships.

It is not without irony that this, the very oldest site in Spain, has, of all ancient Spanish cities, the least remains of antiquity. That is partly due to its later activity and partly to its being a sort of maritime outpost, vulnerable from the sea, filled with commercial activity and peril. At the end of the sixteenth century an English expedition sacked and burned it, and a further fire necessitated its rebuilding. It was rebuilt in regular fashion, as all towns are when they are planned of one piece, in whatever age—unless we except the rebuilding of London, in the next century; and even there very regular plans were laid out by Wren and by Temple. But vested interests were too strong for them, and the old London labyrinth (let us rejoice !) was restored.

Cadiz was rebuilt after a fashion which it is difficult to judge either as insipid or as interesting or as curious : it has been called all these things. It is insipid compared with the intense vitality of the Spanish continuous work, alive with all the past, in city after city of Spanish pride. It is of curious interest compared with any town not Spanish because of the very tall houses, the narrow lanes—narrow for protection from the sun and narrow because the space was so naturally limited—the little turret-like ornaments at the corners of the houses, the swelling of the whole thing up from its walls. All these are curious. Yet I will maintain that the profound interest of Cadiz is not in its whiteness upon the sea wherein, from some way off, you see it reflected very vividly during dead calms ; still less is it in the town's rather meaningless eighteenth-century additions ; nor even in the immemorial oval of its league of wall ; nor in the great legend of Hercules ; but the profound interest of Cadiz lies rather in that secure Bay, the first of the Atlantic harbours.

In a sense you may say that Spain, here in Cadiz, was the mother of all our modern things and of all our looking westward. Cadiz was the first great tidal harbour, filled with the ebb and the flow of the Atlantic and linking us up with the New World.

I have often wished that, in order to make the
story complete, Columbus had sailed from Cadiz
instead of that little anchorage of Saltes, just down
the coast, which has filched from Cadiz an immortal memory. Yet Cadiz reaped the fruits of
that journey, and Cadiz rose and fell thencefor-
ward with the monopoly or the loss, the pro-
ductivity or the slackness, of the American trade.
This it was which made it the victim of foreign
attack. This it was which gave it its vast wealth
in the last period of its power. This it was which
let it sink again in the mid-nineteenth century.
This it is which in part has restored it to-day.

Only in part; for the trade of the world in our
great modern ships now seeks Barcelona. But
Cadiz is the natural entry from the western sea.
It has not the same pride of arms as you will find
in the battling cities of the north. It fell naturally to the Reconquest after the middle of the
thirteenth century. It has few legends of resistance to the Mohammedan power, and, although
you will find Hercules and the two lions carven
above its gates, it is commercial rather than
knightly. But it is the gate from the broad ocean
and from the West, and, alone of the Spanish
cities, it looks directly, uninterruptedly, over its
western horizon at the New Spain beyond.

CHAPTER V

TARRAGONA AND THE CATALANS

I THINK if a man would feel Catalonia he should travel on foot in the northern mountains, hearing the Catalan speech and seeing the Catalan customs upon both sides of the border. Next he should visit for some days one of those smaller towns in which the modern industry of the province, which distinguishes it so sharply from the rest of Spain, has taken root. Lastly, he should steep himself in the spirit of Tarragona.

For Tarragona has that quality which you will everywhere find to be the best preservation of a local genius—the quality of tradition undisturbed by recent activity and expansion. Though it lies in the southernmost part of the province, yet it is intensely Catalan, and sums up in its serene antiquity the traditions of that land.

I have said that the problem of Catalonia and that of Morocco are the two perils of Spain to-day; one might almost say there were no other perils in the path of a continued prosperity, moral and physical. But these two are serious, and there are moments when they seem overwhelming. How serious is that of Morocco, the daily telegrams arriving for years were sufficient to prove. Catalonia is quite another matter. It is not an immediate physical peril, but it is a challenge to the Spanish unity.

The Catalan province, through an accident of history, received a different stamp from that of the rest of the peninsula at a moment when the final characters of our European countrysides were decided during the crystallising process of the Dark Ages. There has resulted not only a very different language—language is a poor test of national definition—but a sharp different corporate spirit and informing local habit.

All the rest of Spain—and Portugal as well for that matter—was moulded and informed by the lengthy, the annealing, the slowly victorious hammering back of Asia from European soil. But Catalonia was the March of the Ebro which Charlemagne kept as a bastion thrown out into Mohammedan land. From the very root of the Dark Ages it remained attached to the Gauls ; and there was a Count of Barcelona to defend the Ebro frontiers of the empire here, just as the Counts and the Margraves upon the Elbe and Danube defended it against the pagan Slavs and Mongols. The broad, open pass of the Cerdagne, the easy passages of the last low eastern hills wherein the Pyrenees fall to the Mediterranean, were gateways into Catalonia at all times ; and the coast country from just south of Narbonne right to the mouths of the Ebro, became one thing.

This separate Catalan idea has never failed. You find it far on in the seventeenth century, when the Catalan Assembly elected Louis XIII. of France to be Count of Barcelona, as a challenge to Madrid (hence the loss to Spain of Perpignan). You find it to-day in the Catalan acceptation of modern industry, and, what is much more important, in the acceptation of those transmontane French ideas, good and evil, which are abhorrent to Aragon and Castille.

Nearly every country of the modern world (with its strong, highly-centralised governments, its rapid communications, its unifying processes of education and law) has some such problem of local resistance to unity. It is not for a foreigner to judge either the moral issues involved or the strength of the forces upon either side, but no view of modern Spain can neglect that anomaly of the Catalonian demand. There is no symptom of decline in it—the local separate spirit is still strong and strengthening ; to judge it, I say, one must not stand in the turmoil and cross-currents of a huge centre like Barcelona, where to some extent the religious quarrel and much more the violent industrial conflict of our time between rich and poor confuse the issue. One must take the Catalonian spirit where it is normal, traditional and native; and you will find it so most in Tarragona.

The town is the most orderly, the most compact, one might say, of all the more living cities of Spain. It is set on the slopes of a high hill, which it exactly covers, and the steep escarpment of which to the east overhangs a vast expanse of sea, over to the unseen Balearics, more than a hundred miles away.

The place has nothing about it of decay, although, like all seats of a peaceful antiquity, it has shrunk greatly from its ancient boundaries. They say that at the height of the Roman power it held, with its slaves and its travellers, a million souls. It has now, with its suburbs, not a twentieth of that number. Yet there does not stand about it that shadow of ancient amplitude which you find round other such cities—Ravenna, or Rome itself—detached relics of ancient use, ruins, the enclosed gardens run wild of palaces long disappeared.

The vineyards and the highly cultivated market ground and the pastures come right up to the limits of its continuous building and to the base of its hill. There seems to have happened here in part what happened wholly to Hippo in Africa; that is, the removal of all the stones, of every trace of building, from the area over which an ancient city shrank; and Tarragona, which gave its name to all these coasts of Spain when the

Roman imperial power was at its height, stands now still marked with all the impress of a capital —but not too large ; exact, dignified, and with no touch of mourning, of death, or even of decay. The port, which seems so small to our modern eyes, and which was yet the making of this centre over against the coasts of Italy, lies at its foot with a modern quarter around it. From this flat arises the hill of the city, which you mount by a main street, or better, by a fine flight of steps upon the seaward side, which climb right up to the broad parapet-way and garden, overhanging the Mediterranean upon the height ; and there it is, upon the very summit of the hill, that you find the heart of the city and its memories. There you will see, built by chance into the walls of private houses, the stones of fifteen hundred and two thousand years.

I came upon one most curious window in a wall of no pretensions. Its two sides were supported by two red slabs, memorials or tombs, still inscribed with Latin letters. The lintel above was of a different colour, a greyish white, which looked much older, but was, in fact, more recent, and may, in fact, have counted not more than a thousand years. It had been taken, I suppose, from some ruined synagogue, for it bore, deeply cut into the hard, rough substance of it, a run of Hebrew letters.

Such things meet you, I had almost said, at

every turn in these very steep, turning ways of the upper city; and you see, side by side with them, the good and sober modern buildings, still rich with tradition, in which the Spaniards everywhere excel.

Upon the very height of the summit, where once the citadel stood (closely surrounded by the immense blocks, older than history, of the cyclopean wall), stands the cathedral ; and though every town of the Peninsula centres on its church, and therefore makes every mention of each particular shrine something of a repetition, no one can write of, or remember, Tarragona save in terms of that astonishing thing.

It stands more lonely than the main churches of most of the other towns, for it is at the extremity and on the height of the whole city. A wide space before its approach, flooded with an intense light and commonly empty of men, is your introduction to something exceptional in your travels. For as you pass the doors you come suddenly out of the glare into a very cold, black void. At first you can see nothing. You are in what seems to be the complete darkness of a vast cavern, very wide and as icy as might be some subterranean refuge ; violently contrasting in its sudden cold and empty depth of night with the torrid splendour outside.

Then, very gradually, the eye perceives a glimmering shaft, an altar cloth under the gleam

45

of a small taper ; a broad vault lost above. But nothing more. The mediæval architects of Catalonia delighted in the two effects of gloom and breadth : a breadth which seems beyond the capacity of stone ; an arch which seems, in the gloaming, almost too flat for so great a span. It is here at Tarragona only an extreme degree of what you also have in the chief parish church, and still more in the cathedral, of Barcelona. That degree of breadth is indeed so extreme that this strange, cubic nave of Tarragona, ebony night when you come into it out of the sunlight, stands by itself, and has no true parallel elsewhere in Europe. They who built it desired a place wherein the soul of man should enter at once into a profound contemplation, and be wholly cut off from the consideration of external things. They desired to put over and around the soul of man, roofing him and guarding him all about, a mystery of silence and of immensity. Certainly they achieved what they desired. I could imagine some man, over-experienced in the noisy unmeaning of the world—its ambitions bought at ten times their worth, and lost in a moment, its futile, torturing friction, and its fruitless, wasted fevers of energy—coming many hundred miles to find this place again, and to rest. It is the very heart of final repose.

When the eye has slowly grown used to the dim details of this huge cave and has begun to see its

46

sublime proportion and design, it has another fulness of experience before it in the cloisters through the northern door, close on the gospel side of the great altar.

Passing through this northern door you come to what is the most charming, the most blessed, of all the wild gardens of the world, framed in a quadrilateral of delicate arches all around. I know them all, the cloisters of the Middle Ages. Here in England, every one, and I think every one in France; and here, in Spain, I know Barcelona, Seville, Ovideo and the strange double tier of Ripoll; and Leon, where I thought I had found, fifteen years ago, the loveliest of all such seclusions. But the cloister of Tarragona far surpasses them all. Upon its walls stand Roman tombs and, of course, the memories of the Middle Ages, and in one place, an exquisite small Moorish window, chiselled to an infinity of detail; and in another, a small rough monstrous head, from the ends of our darkness, when sculpture was almost lost. All the centuries are about you, but all asleep; and the only life of the place is in the graceful solemnity of the few trees, the grass and flowers of the court, the birds shooting to and fro, high round the warm golden stones of the tower.

That sky, that air you breathe, that slight wind coming over those ancient roofs are all of the sea. You know as you sit there, in the shade of the

47

northern cloister, looking at that very mellow tower, kindly against the intense noon sky, and as your eye finds nothing but that sky, with the tiles of the garth and the chancel roof against it, that behind you, unseen, is a great regiment of mountains, guarding the plain and looking on this abrupt lonely hill, which is your station ; and you know that just beyond, down below the giant walls, at the foot of the steeply-falling slope, is the splendour of the Mediterranean. All the while there is no sound but the very slight murmur of the sea wind in the leaves of the lonely little garden and, at long spaces, the sharp note of a darting bird.

It sounds an odd thing to say of eager Catalonia —but it is true—that here, if anywhere in the world, there is peace. That word, which the young cannot understand, but which represents, after a certain age, all the hunger of the heart, has here taken on flesh, as it were—a flesh of stone— and is with us : peace incarnate.

CHAPTER VI

SALAMANCA

O F the towns in Europe which, by the sound of their names and by the connotation of them, coupled with their remoteness, carry influence, Salamanca is one.

Such a glamour is commonly disappointing in experience. Either the place was once worthy of the verbal symbol which stands for it in a foreign ear but has been destroyed by modern travel, or it has been swallowed up (like Barcelona) by the modern industrial development and has but a nucleus of strong things, standing small and half forgotten in a flood of modern worthlessness. Now Salamanca is different from these, for it is worthy of its name.

I had always desired to see it, but I never had. In the days when I wandered on foot over northern Spain as a younger man I never pushed so far west. Later the main line to Madrid (which all follow) held me, as it does the elderly. I have found that most of those who go under the walls of the city upon their way to Lisbon pass it unseen; the International Express runs by it, but does not leave visitors. Like so many of the finest things in Europe, it is seen from the railway at its worst. When I did come to visit Salamanca the other day for the first time in my life I found it, as I say, worthy of all that it had promised. But to judge it as it should be judged, one must not come in by the common road or rail from the direction of north or east. One must come in across the river from the south.

The great University of the Middle Ages, the rival of Oxford and of Paris, the dominating towers, the characteristic saffron stone of the hill —all these stand out before you on the journey northward from the Guadarrama mountains.

I had not myself the good fortune to approach it in this fashion, but I shall take that road next time I come to the city, for it is from the end of that road, coming to the River Tormes and its ancient bridge, that you see Salamanca as it was meant to be seen—a pyramid of great buildings culminating in the towering mass of the cathedral.

Here, as in a hundred other cases, it is from the Roman approach that one sees the European meaning. The road, thus coming upon Salamanca northward from the mountains, was, and is, Roman. The bridge over which that road reaches the city (coming in at the foot of its low cliff) is the bridge over which the Roman armies marched—which the Roman armies made. Its stones are still Roman, and the strength of them.

You may say that all the central and northern

CATHEDRAL AND ROMAN BRIDGE, SALAMANCA.

To face page 50.

famous towns of Spain, the towns of the upland, of the plateau (especially of Old and New Castille), have a note of isolation. They stand on great wind-swept open places, with only here and there a tree, and only here and there, miles apart, each from each, little groups of houses. But Salamanca has this character more strongly impressed upon it than has any other town—this quality of loneliness and the surprising imprint of a special life in the midst of things unlike itself.

You come upon Salamanca as you might come upon a human traveller in a place where you expected no man. It stands in the midst of what in autumn might be thought a desert—what, even when the crops are green in spring, has a fine desolation about it ; and that desolation is made the more striking by the line of snow-tipped, rocky heights to the south, which horizon the plains along the sky. One would think those plains waterless as one goes the miles across them, but one comes not infrequently upon their rivers running in broad trenches scooped out of the loose soil, or breaking through reefs of barren limestone ; rivers which vary in volume from great tumbles of water when the snow is melting, or after storm, to mere runnels between sand banks in the late summer heat or in the depth of the exceedingly cold winters of that tableland. All such rivers lend their value to the towns upon them. For, different as such rivers are from our northern broad and equal streams, with their green meadows, and different as they are even from the mountain streams of Italy, yet are the Spanish towns upon them river towns. Toledo is the town of the Tagus, Saragossa of the Ebro, Salamanca of the Tormes.

Wherever great wealth has been centred in the past upon some restricted site, if there has accompanied its expenditure a civilisation of high spiritual value and of a fixed, exalted sense of beauty, you have the works of man in a profusion of creative power fixed for ever. You will see that effect in the neglected square half-mile of Santiago, crammed with magnificence, and you see it here in Salamanca.

The University Buildings have what all the ancient universities of Europe have—a vitality bequeathed to them by generations of youth. In the private houses of Salamanca you see before you, in stone, endeavour and accumulated effort, an expenditure of carving without limit, an attempt everywhere to leave a record, and that attempt successful.

But it is the cathedral, more than any other building, which gives its soul to the place. And in it you may note what is the characteristic of Spain—that the decay of the Middle Ages did not affect (as one might think it should have done) the skill of men's hands nor the justice of their vision.

Salamanca   Rozli are   28 May 1920

SALAMANCA AND THE GUADARRAMA.

To face page 53.

The ornament is late; the piling on of detail is of a sort which tourists in the Ruskin tradition will call excessive. There are experiments in structure which are manifestly exaggerated. Yet the whole is a marvel.

I think it especially characteristic of the place that in the frieze which runs round the nave for a total distance of perhaps three hundred yards (a crowd of little figures, animals and foliage and men, one creation from first to last) each detail is an individual; just as in real creation each living unit has its own life. It is not enough to say there is no repetition; it is rather true to say there is infinite variety in unity.

Also have I seen in the church of Salamanca, better than elsewhere, success in the attaining of *height* and its effect in the noble ironwork. The soaring gates of the chapels are as tall as the masts of a full-rigged ship. The pilasters, coloured and even (what may seem excessive, but on the spot is sober enough) *gilt*, have almost the effect of Beauvais in their ceaseless uplifting of line. Moreover, less than in any other Spanish cathedral I know does the Coro break the effect of height.

The cathedral of Salamanca is a splendid edifice from within and from without. It has that power of using the features in its landscape which the men of its time gave to every great building. It is the true completion of the height on which it stands, leading up into its tower the lines of the hill which is its foundation.

Lastly there is this to be said about my old city of Salamanca—something which lends a peculiar pleasure to the visiting of it—that it is not mournful in its decay ; it is not abandoned ; it is properly alive.

Its schools, which were one of the four great groups of the Western World hold not a quarter of the youth they once held. It does not radiate, as once it radiated, its intelligence and learning through the West. But it is not dead nor even diminished in life ; it is still the great university town, it is still a national glory, and, what is more important, it is still itself, its function is not warped. Its value is permanent, its essential activity unimpaired, and all this is crowned with permanent beauty, like a garment, not new at all, but never to fade.

Salamanca · Edmund L. Warre

CASA DA CONCHA, SALAMANCA.

To face page 54.

Part II
Portugal

CHAPTER VII

VIZEU

IT has been said of England that if a foreign traveller, having but a few days in which to see the place, were to travel through the South from Dover through Salisbury to Devon, he would have seen a certain country. If he were to land in the Humber, and travel through the Yorkshire industrial towns and the Lancashire ones to Liverpool, he would have seen one so different that he could hardly believe himself to have been in the same State as that of which the first was a part.

The contrast in Portugal between the sea plain and the hills is nothing like so strong, for in England we have our world sharply divided between that old traditional aspect, dating back at least to the fifteenth century, and the monstrous ash and black ruin of the nineteenth-century industrialism.

Nevertheless, of Portugal it may be said that if a man only knows the sea plain he cannot judge the country. If he only knew the hills he might hardly suspect the towns and the sea plain. Of the hills it would seem (from what those who have long known the country tell me) Vizeu is the typical, small, dignified market town, bishopric, and the rest. I suppose that if a man had but one place to visit in which he should desire to see what the hill country of Portugal and its people were like, he could not do better than choose this one example of Vizeu for his experiment.

Whether it be climate, or some preservation of race through difficulty of access, the hill country of Portugal far more resembles in people and habit (and somewhat even in natural exterior) certain parts of France and England, than that belt along the Atlantic upon which was poured in the past the sudden new wealth of the country during its great adventure of the late Middle Ages. There is in Vizeu (that typical town of the Portuguese hills) a calm and a recollection, a sober way of living, a neatness and an evidence of active toil which we of the North do not connect with the culture of the South. I came into Vizeu through Mondalgue, and there were moments on the road when one might have thought oneself in the Parisis : moments of old walls and close villages and tall trees, thick grass, all of which made one think of Northern homes rather than of the South.

And, indeed, this approach to Portugal clearly explains to the traveller how the country came to be separate in its modern history from the rest of the Peninsula, and why an intense national feeling

VIZEU : PORTUGAL : COLONNADE OF GRAO-VASCO MUSEUM.

To face page 58.

arose which defied the artificial union with Spain three hundred years ago, and welcomed the restoration of a national dynasty as strongly as any of the far more recalcitrant nationalities of the North have welcomed their freedom.

For one drops off from the hot arid plateaux of Castille (steppes stretching for two or three days' journey before the eye, beneath the distant and barren ridges of their Sierras), on to the well-watered, fertile, tree-clad slopes of the Portuguese hills, through a distinct belt of something very like stony desert.

The main road, the railway, each goes through more than a day's journey—more than thirty miles, indeed more than fifty—of huge granite boulders and sparse cracked oak groves—such groves getting rarer and rarer, with little or no water, rare scrubby tufts of grass, few huts, no fields.

This belt of quasi-desert forms, as it were, the edge of the tableland, and is carried on over the edge to the beginning of the Atlantic slope.

Then one comes, quite rapidly, on a change. Vineyards appear. The woods cascade, one wave below the other, down the hillsides, and there is flowing water at their feet. You see below you ridge upon ridge of dense forest-land falling far and steeply towards the ocean, and you begin to pass into places of wealth and security, and the well-founded habitations of men.

59

It is a very striking contrast. Every borderland in Europe explains itself and has its
geographical meaning (the borderland between
England and Scotland always seems to me when
I cross it to explain the different historical
directions of the two countries) ; but the marshes
of Portugal, as you enter them from the high
plains of old Castille, the desert of rock boulders
on the edge of that two thousand foot tableland
as you fall rapidly from it into the warm and
damp Atlantic belt below, are a more visible
natural frontier than you may find elsewhere, save
in the great mountain ranges.

Of that foot-hill country Vizeu, as I have said,
is a natural, though small, capital. It seems to
have come into existence as a fortress on a tiny
scale. Even the modern town (of the humble
size of one of our smaller cathedral towns),
stretches far beyond the quadrilateral of huge
primitive stones which was the original stronghold. It got its name perhaps as a 'look-out,' for
to the north it covers a wide landscape. It got its
use undoubtedly from its possibilities for defence.

Of this past, the remaining stamp here, as
in most of the older towns of Europe, is the
cathedral. It is on the scale of all the rest of
the place, quite small ; built, one would say, for
a township of not five hundred families, but
having about it in its overlooking of the steeps
to the north and east, in the thickness of its walls,

60

VIZEU

VIZEU : THE CLOISTER BETWEEN CATHEDRAL AND
MUSEUM.

To face page 60.

in the airy height of its upper cloister walk, the marks of a mountain citadel.

On that building a man might spend ten days, examining its spirit. Here, as in the great sister far away, Narbonne, the choir sings from a stage high above the people ; not a choir of special singers, but the choir of the Chapter itself, the Canons. Here, as in certain other towns of the South, strong wood is married with stone, and the wood impresses upon the stone itself a certain quality. For instance, the ornaments to the roof, though stone, are carved with the freedom of wood, and ropes (in stone) are carried everywhere throughout the vaults, carved into knots.

The people of the place have gathered into the cloisters and the rooms adjoining curiosities, a few treasures which the bishopric retained. One very fine *Tu es Petrus* of the early Flemish Renaissance and half a dozen others—good pictures which nobody knows ; a mass of earthenware statuary and the more remarkable carved wooden statuary. Indeed, the glory of Portugal is its mass of luxuriant wood carving, and nowhere will you see this better, though on a small scale, than at Vizeu.

More than the town itself is the land about it, deep forest valleys and their streams ; and any one wishing to find the true life of Portugal, apart from the coast (which does not sufficiently represent the country), should seek it here, in the hills.

61

CHAPTER VIII

OPORTO

I FANCY that every strange town, coming to the traveller's eyes for the first time, creates within him some effect for which he was not at all prepared by any part of his reading. There is always something about it (to him, at least, an overwhelming characteristic) which had not been expressed in any one of the general descriptions. This is not, I suppose, because the various places too well known in European travel do not affect others as they affect oneself, but rather that print creates a habit of ceaseless repetition upon one model.

Now Oporto has in my eyes, since I have seen it, such a characteristic which I had not noticed in any description of the many I had come across ; a characteristic which struck me with violence the first time I set eyes on it. It is this : that it lies in the depths of a chasm.

The port is on a mountain river, deep down between two banks which fall towards it so steeply as to make a gorge rather than a valley. I know of only one other place where a port of some size has such a situation, and that is New-

VIEW UP THE DOURO. A BRUNEL BRIDGE AND WELLINGTON'S FORD
BEYOND THE BEND.

To face page 62.

castle-upon-Tyne : but though Newcastle also gives this effect of a gorge or trench (and the height of its bridge above the river has thus impressed every etcher and painter of it), the effect is nothing like so strong as it is at Oporto. One wonders, as one comes in from the south, how such a confined waterway ever came to be used from the outer sea, and it is only when one gets down towards the level of it that one appreciates its width.

Oporto is only one more example of those land gates from the sea which, having struck root under older and simpler conditions of smaller ships and of lesser human gatherings, continue, by the necessity of their inheritance, a role which they would not fulfil had they to begin their service to-day. Oporto must have begun in the old Roman times, or even before then, as some small cluster of little warehouses and shippers' exchanges upon the narrow shelf of its river bank ; not yet climbing up the very steep bank behind, and dealing only with few vessels of small draught and of light burden.

It could have had no great trade before the discovery of land in and beyond the Atlantic. It had no highly specialised function to support before the development of the English wine trade during the last two and a half centuries. The modern world has compelled its partial abandonment. The larger ships have to make land at Leixões, an artificial harbour built out upon the Atlantic coast, north of the river mouth, and exposed to the south-westerly winds. Yet the ancient function of the town itself as a port has survived : just as London, made by London Bridge, has to accommodate its main shipping far down the river, but keeps its commercial centre on the old sites north of the Pool.

The Douro valley carries this character of a gorge or trench eastward for some days' journey inland : as men see who go up on foot, or in a boat against the stream, until they come to the Spanish frontier.

Of all the great Spanish rivers, which fall from the high tablelands on to the sea plain, this one, the Douro, is the most rapid, turbulent and mountainous ; and the soil through which it cuts, the earth which nourishes those famous vineyards (a small and narrow patch of golden land), is friable, sawn away by the violence of the water, as is soft wood by steel. Hence the ravine before the mouth of which, and upon the steep banks of which, the town stands.

Oporto has grown out to surmount two hills with something of a subsidiary valley between. It is marked everywhere by the activity which the English trade has given it. From this has it derived its wealth. This is its meaning in the political geography of Europe.

Everywhere the impress of England is dis-

OPORTO
Pedro Villarte
June 1926

FOUNTAIN ON THE RAMPED PATHWAY TO THE CATHEDRAL, OPORTO.

To face page 64.

coverable. The memorable ford where Wellington crossed ; the famous ' Factory,' which is the
noble old stone house of the English wine
merchants ; the great English names of the trade
—all these are marks of Oporto.

There is about this strong link between England
and a distant foreign town something exceptional
which you will not find anywhere else in Europe ;
yet there is no impress of English art or English
thought upon the place such as you may discover
in French districts where, during the later Middle
Ages, the English crown had direct rule. There
are pieces of church architecture in Bordeaux
which are distinctively English. Here and there
in Normandy you will find characteristics of
fifteenth-century England left by the passage of
Henry V., and by the minority of his son. Bay-
onne cathedral might be known for a relic of the
old Plantagenet connection even though we had
lost all record of its building. But Oporto, save
for the factory, which is strong eighteenth-century
English, has not such architectural marks : and
it is singular that this should be so.

They told me in the course of my visit that in
the old records of the place, and in diaries and
letters of Englishmen before the days of steam-
ships, there is perpetual reference to the ' Bar '—
and no wonder ! The Bar of the Douro is one
of the most remarkable things I have seen. It is
not merely silted up with a great expanse of sand

which almost forbids entry—that is common to scores and hundreds of rivers. It is not merely that this great bar shifts, as do such bars in such places, exposed to great storms from the Atlantic. It is rather that immediately *within* the fairway, just after a boat has made good its entry into quiet water, you still find unexpected rocks menacing the way, and considerable patches of shifting sand.

The site of the place (two thousand yards below the wharves of the town) emphasises that truth about Oporto which the eyes grasp from the first moment of seeing its profound valley—that it was originally a little dangerous haven, hardly to be entered from the sea, uncertain, not to be used on a large scale, yet turned at last by the activity of man into a place far beyond its powers. Oporto is an excellent proof of the truth that if physical geography moulds history on its largest lines, yet, in all the passing developments of history, it is man that turns nature to his use rather than nature controls man. The huge iron bridge (of English design and construction) spanning the whole gorge at so vast a height, the unnatural climbing up of the houses from height to height, the exiguous stream, its violence, its difficult entry, the necessity for a new modern port wholly of man's provision, are all witnesses to that same dominance of man's will over earth.

When the Northerners began fighting their way down, pushing the Mohammedans south-

THE BISHOPS' PALACE, OPORTO.

To face page 66.

wards, this little Roman place being called essentially 'The Port' (its name is Porto, and it is
an error that *we* should have called it 'Oporto,'
the Port) gave its name to all that followed. It
was the 'Porto Calle'; it created the general
name of 'Portugal.'

Part III
The Recovered Country

CHAPTER IX

ISLAM AND CHRISTENDOM

THERE is a section of Western Europe, of the Western Roman Empire, which suffered a peculiar fate. It was deeply wounded by Asia, and but slowly recovered from the wound. The period of Asia's dominance is already half forgotten among the Northern peoples—it is a story of so long ago ; and it seems done with. Yet indirectly the great struggle between Islam and Christendom is still moulding all our lives. Half the wealth and half the classical tradition of the Mediterranean were swamped by the enemies of our culture and of our European soul ; half our civilisation was drowned under a Mohammedan deluge. The land of St. Augustine, the land of Meleager, the land of the Iliad, and the land of the Incarnation. The surge overran the islands of the sea—Sicily, the Balearics, and the rest ; it roared up to the very foot-hills of the Pyrenees, its furthest foam passed Poitiers, and it looked for some hundreds of years as though the old and strong foundation which Greece and Rome had laid, and our Christendom which is their flower and fruit, would be destroyed.

The assault was sudden, and immensely successful; the counter-attack abominably painful, strenuous, uncertain, only most gradually making good. The Asiatics charged in one long lifetime over all the marble of the ancient world in North Africa, in Spain; cut off the great roads and the secure Roman law, and the landed system, and everything else that had made Europe Europe. But to reconquer even part of that land, to beat Islam back to the desert again upon even one sector has taken a thousand years.

Spain was recovered, in countless fluctuating cavalry charges, advances and checks, sieges, and raids: the islands, in daring sea adventures; Barbary—what to-day we call Tunis, Algiers and Morocco—only in our own time. To-day we look on the result of these struggles much as a man looks upon the wreckage revealed at low water upon a seashore flooded and wrecked at high tide under a storm.

In that enormous conflict the Europe we know was born. Out of the discipline of that conflict arose our military spirit, our loyalties, and our ballads. This beating back of the Mohammedan was the training ground of all our peoples Northern as well as Southern—for the recruits poured in from every side. It was in the heat of such a furnace, in the press of the Crusades, that we found our characteristic architecture, which has stamped all Europe with the pointed arch, our representative system (now in decay)—for parliaments are from the Pyrenees—our national monarchies, and that common loyalty to Europe which is to-day half forgotten, but which any menace immediately revives.

Any one who looks at the history of Christendom sees this armed debate with Islam as the fundamental and determining thing. We beat off the Pagan of the North and of the East— Mongol, Scandinavian and the rest—in the Dark Ages. We assured ourselves on that side, and we had raised the siege against those barbaric besiegers before the year 1000. We had beaten them to their knees in battle ; tamed them and baptised them ; brought them to heel and to school. But Islam was another matter. It was not pagan ; it was a perversion of our own creed. It was not barbaric ; it had more learning and better arts than we. It enjoyed our scholarship through its Greek subjects, and lived by a strange, warped adaptation of our own culture. Its fierce appeal to human equality and to justice, the simplicity of its doctrine, had captured great masses of our own people who continued to work for it and to support it.

The recovery of provinces lost to so powerful an enemy occupied the energies of Christian men for thirty generations ; nor is their task yet accomplished.

In this struggle the combatants upon both sides

73

of the Mediterranean were for a time exhausted. The extreme north, which had taken but little part in the tremendous affair, had the advantages of a half-neutral; it lost less blood, and could boast on that account greater reserves of energy, which it still enjoys. But those who had been on the fighting line of the struggle achieved that by which we live. The men who recovered Spain and Sicily and the Balearics, who perpetually challenged the pirate ports of Barbary, who stood to arms, century after century, upon the fluctuating frontier between the Mass and the Koran—these were the men who not only permitted Europe to survive, but who gave it its permanent character.

The belt which they recovered, which they reconquered, bears everywhere stamped upon it the signs of this millenary battle. Thus, there has been a destruction of trees in all that zone. Islam was the enemy of the tree. Where the Mohammedan conquest remained there was no re-afforesting; the wood was cut down and not replaced. A sort of bareness, which is like a phantasm of the desert, stretches to this day over all those lands which the great Mohammedan tide submerged; and it is now with difficulty and most painfully, tardily, insufficiently that Europe is attempting to re-afforest those lands which were so shaded and full of pasture in the great classic times.

You may stand on the mountain walls of Castro
Giovanni in Sicily and look down, half a mile
below, upon the fields where the King of the
Dark Places surprised Persephone. Those fields
were famous for their groves and their flowers in
the old time; to-day you have nothing before you
and below you but the burned and naked earth.

The tide of alien conquest makes a sort of high-
water mark all along the Mediterranean lands ; a
line to be traced by the ruin of the greenery and
by the incursion everywhere up to its limits of
the blasting, southern, desert air.

But there is much more than this to mark the
battlefield. Throughout that world you may
discover, in a myriad details of human effort, the
three great strata remaining.

First comes that of the old Mediterranean
civilisation from which we all descend, the Roman
and Greek world. The columns of its temples,
the tiers of its amphitheatres, the great flags of
its roads, the Roman-Greek town with its forum,
the Roman or Greek name degraded and transformed : all are there.

Next above come the centuries of Islam; the
Mosque and the minaret, the bulging dome, the
waisted horseshoe arch, all that Islam adapted
from the later Greek world and touched with its
own spirit ; the perpetual intricacy of pattern,
the vivid delicacy of colour, the worship of
seclusion and silence.

75

Then you get the laſt, superimposed, layer of
Europe returning. Our Gothic in the place of
their horseshoe arch, our Roman script in the
place of their Arabic script, which is but debased
Greek, our maſterful ſtonework in the place of
their weak plaſter, our permanence in the place
of their ephemeral though burning moods. You
get the cathedral of Palma in Majorca, ſtanding
out like a fortress into the sea ; or the cathedral
of Seville, perhaps the nobleſt of human achieve-
ments, ſtill overlooking that Moorish court which
was the entry to the Mosque the Chriſtian church
has replaced.

Indeed, the Giralda, the Bell Tower of Seville,
is the very symbol of the combat and victory.
The main shaft was of Islam. I have already
written of its counterpart which ſtill ſtands over
the sea in Morocco by Rabat, called there ' the
Tower of Hassan.' But the Giralda bears a
Christian top, and is the belfry of that cathedral
which is the greateſt monument we have in
Chriſtendom, of Chriſtendom, to-day.

From the victory of Lepanto onwards you get
the recovery of the Roman and the Greek spirit
in the lines of ſtone impressed upon the Mohammedan detail beneath, and at laſt, all our modern
grandeurs and folly of ironwork, of great ports
thruſting long arms into the sea, of solid, dull,
official buildings ; our machines, our roads, our
commerce, our vices and our triumphs, are now

76

THE TOWER OF THE GIRALDA, SEVILLE.

To face page 76.

imposed upon that which once had so nearly defeated us. Rome has taken root again from Carthage to the Atlantic.

Therein lies the profound appeal of all the recovered country and its towns. In Palermo, in Palma, in the ruined Roman towns of Timgad, Lamboesis, Volubilis, Leptis and a score of others; in the still continuing towns such as Constantine; in the transformed old centres such as Sousse, you see before your eyes in a vividly apparent pattern the interweaving of those three great epochs of our race. You have present to the sight that antiquity wherein the Christian church was founded; then the new, thin, piercing spirit of the Mohammedan horseman; then the re-entry of Europe.

It is in the buildings, the dress, the very animals, the landscape, is that triple contrast, that triple stratification. Nowhere else in the world, I think, does history still remain alive, so tangible, visible : two thousand years of it.

You stand on the huge stones of a coliseum at sunrise, seeing nothing but the mass of an enormous Roman theatre, and between you and the sky only distant, burning, white mountains and the flats of the sea. You turn, and at your side is the costume of Islam; you walk into the evening and find yourself in the modern French streets of Tunis.

In succeeding chapters I will discuss this land

77

that Islam has dominated, picking out particular points where a man may see, side by side, the three eras of our race ; its founding, its peril, and its triumph.

So strong still is the subtle remaining influence of Islam, that you find it far up north, in a wall of Tarragona, in the gateway of a Saragossan building, in a popular word of the Pyrenees. So enduring is the older Roman foundation which we, its descendants, have restored, that you may watch the Mohammedan peasant in his market bargaining in the Arabic words of the old invasion, but using in his talk the terms of the French currency and of French weights and measures of to-day ; and that market is held in the forum of a Roman town, with the pillars of the temples of the gods overlooking the Berber as he moves. He drives his cattle to market by great roads which modern Europe has made, he registers his purchase in the European offices of the new governors. If he is well-to-do he drives off home in one of those new horseless machines of ours. But at sunset, he lifts up his hands in prayer from his fields, a ritual of Islam.

In those towns where the religion of Islam has at last died—the Spanish, the Sicilian, the Balearic towns—yet is the spirit of Islam chiselled and carved in everywhere, marking the whole.

In the countrysides where the Mohammedan conquest was complete, the majestic ruins of the

THE TOMB OF THE ALCAZAR, SEVILLE.

To face page 78.

Roman World stand clearest. There is nothing of classic antiquity more living than these still remaining colonnades, triumphal arches, aqueducts, theatres; Segovia, Cherchell, El Djem. It is more arresting to see these survivals of Rome on the African and Spanish soil than in northern Italy or Provence, in Verona, or in Pola, or in Nîmes; for in Africa and Spain the Roman ruins were not cherished by a continuous culture. They survive as heroic veterans which stood the storm and outlived it until the descendants of their builders returned.

CHAPTER X

CEFALU

O N the northern shore of Sicily, well westward of its midmost point, stands a rock
and a town which may be taken for the
type of the reconquered lands. These are the
rock and the town of Cefalu.

All that coast is a procession of enormous
headlands, Gibraltars of their kind thrown out
against the seas, Corfano, Pellegrino and a score
of others. But among them the rock of Cefalu
is pre-eminent in its savage isolation, its defence,
its bold challenge and the antiquity of its appeal
to man. On the crags of its summit—I know not
how high above the harbour, perhaps a thousand
feet, perhaps twelve hundred—the first most
ancient city, far older than any record, held its
secure state ; inexpugnable ; looking down from
its walls upon precipice every way. A few blocks
of its enormous monuments remain and a trace
of its wall. A little hook of reef, a narrow strand,
provided a sufficient refuge and approach from
the sea, thence a made path and steps of stone
led up the sheer to the inhabited summit.

This, the first destiny of Cefalu and cause of its

THE ROCK AND TOWN OF CEFALU.

To face page 80.

settlement, its place as a fortress, was renewed
time and again all down its incalculable history,
it certainly will reappear when the next phase of
confusion and decline shall fall upon civilisation.
But with the Roman peace the high town was
abandoned and the city stretched along the belt
of shore, the sloping foot of the huge crag. The
town left the summit and gathered round its
little harbour, strung upon either side of the coast
track which leads from the Straits of Messina to
the last eastern cape of the island by Trapani.
There has it since remained, clinging to the sea-
fringe of its towering cube of stone, forgetting
its first cyclopean foundation above.

All the ebb and flow of the East and the West
have passed over it. Greece gave it its headland
name. Carthage ruled it : Rome wrested it
away. In the height of the Dark Ages—perhaps
before the death of Charlemagne—Islam had
planted a garrison here and made it an outpost in
that sweeping of the Mediterranean whereby the
Mohammedan and his Asia so nearly overwhelmed us. The Saracen chieftains, quarrelling
among themselves, let in the Norman adventurers, the men from the Cotentin, who had set
out to seize these lands a lifetime before the
Crusades. It was with them that the recovery of
Cefalu by the Christian West began, and from
them that Cefalu received the great building and
the shrine which is its mark to-day and has

dignified it during nearly eight hundred years
For it was here that Roger of Sicily, the Norman
King, driving landward in a storm, ordered to be
set up in his name the church which he had vowed
to build in whatever place should harbour him,
if he should save his life and come to land.   He
devoted revenue largely to his vow, and thus it
is that there stands in Sicily to-day a cathedral of
the North, one of the very earliest to depend upon
the pointed arch, large, of one kind : with superb
mosaic looking not a lifetime old, but set into its
cement before Richard of England sailed by with
his square crimson sails to conquer Cyprus and
to fail before Jerusalem.

That mosaic is as vivid a witness to history as
you could find in all the South, or in any part of
the recovered lands.   Here is an art that was the
glory of the later Empire before the generals
revolted and began those disorders of the last
Roman armies in which Rome was sacked,
Britain lost, Africa cut off for a time and Gaul left
derelict under a local commander of auxiliaries.
The mosaic, with its eternal quality, remained,
the characteristic of those church walls on which
the Christian Emperor impressed permanent
record.   It is the art of Justinian as of Theodosius.
It is the sign manual of that restoration of our
culture which the genius of Belisarius effected
in the West and which Islam came so near to
destroying.

CEFALU : EAST END OF THE CATHEDRAL.

To face page 82.

Islam swept over Sicily. Its chaos ruled. It began the massacre of the forests, the desiccation of the soil. The towns decayed, and their crafts. The Norman order and Christendom brought back a spirit not of that climate, but of the North. Yet here, in the most typically Norman of all Sicilian things, the not-Norman, the Byzantine mosaic returns, appearing again above the retreat of the Saracenic flood and set in the frame of that Ogive which means for us rather Chartres, Canterbury and Notre Dame than anything of Byzantium or of Ravenna.

All the apse is filled with it : sombre purples, a few deep reds, and innumerable squares in a sheet of glittering gold. The great subject is Christ in Judgment, the Heroic Face that dominates all the nave from above. He holds in His right hand the Open Book of record, His left is raised for acquittal or sentence. Below this head, with its not mortal proportions, are fixed upon the square space, above the altar, the lesser figures of the twelve apostles ; and the whole, I say, seems to be of yesterday, or of our fathers' time at the most, so living is the surface. Yet it has looked down upon Christian men for more than seven centuries. May the evils of a coming time spare it !

Around that Head and Face, upon either side, following the border of the pointed arch of the roof (the true equilateral of the first Gothic) runs in legible, large, square script, lighter against a darker ground, the noblest motto yet found for the Judge and Redeemer and Brother of mankind. It was the sight of this motto which inspired Sargent to what is, undoubtedly, the highest, by far the highest, monument of his genius—the work in the public library of Boston, showing the fall of the old gods and centred upon such a treatment of the Crucifixion as one would have thought no modern man had it in him to create. But Sargent created it, thus inspired from Cefalu.

The motto runs thus :

' Factus homo factor hominis factique redemptor
Judico corporeus corpora corda Deus.'

An hexameter and a pentameter, with the characteristic internal rhyme of the second. And it means ' I, having been made Man, and being the Maker of Man, and the Redeemer of what I made, judge in bodily form the bodies and the hearts of man : for I am God.'

But Sargent in his masterpiece changed one word for the sake of his subject—this being not the Christ in Judgment, but the Christ crucified. He changed ' Judico ' to ' Redimo '—writing ' I redeem ' for ' I judge.' A transposition was necessary, also, for the sake of the metre, so that the motto to Sargent's Christ on the Cross at Boston reads :

' Factus homo factor hominis factique redemptor
Corporeus redimo corpora corda Deus.'

CEFALU : THE MOSAIC OF THE APSE.

To face page 84.

I think his genius to discover, and to be inspired by, such lines was as great as that which produced his painting.

Such, then, is Cefalu, crammed with the ages. It may be asked whether nothing is left here to mark their passage except this effect of the Norman married with the Imperial mosaic of Constantinople: nothing Saracenic or Greek and Roman?

I saw nothing—save fragments, on a shoulder of the hill, of a castle built there in the Middle Ages and on the bare summit against the sky a few huge boulders of the town before history.

There was not here in Cefalu that desire to fill every bare space with detail, nor that occasional hint at a pinched curve which reveals an Arabian spirit in Palermo, nor any of that perspective of crowded arches round a small, cool court which, in the Benedictine cloister of that town, reminds one oddly of the African palaces oversea. There was no delight in that excessive involution of line, that chipping of surface into fret and cusp which workmen once occupied on Saracenic walls and domes with difficulty forgot when they dealt later with the Christian shrines. In the outer lines of the cathedral, in the body of the building there is only the Northern spirit, with squat towers that might have come from Lisieux or Coutances; and within, there is that tradition of tessellated wall-picturing, a Christ that might have come from the Bosphorous.

It was very strange to observe, against the dark of the choir, a transept capital which, at a distance, seemed Corinthian, but which, close at hand, was a cluster of grotesques : monsters and monkeys. It was strange, under the eyes of such a Face as that which looked down upon us from the eastern roof, to see a baptismal font supported by the fierce leopards of the Dark Ages, the mythology of Anjou and Maine, the things men imagined during the long wars against the heathens of the North Sea, before Europe awoke to the noise and splendour of the Crusades.

Such is Cefalu : the weight of its nave and apse is prodigious above the town and against the Mediterranean. It had, before it left fame and drew apart from the story of Europe, one great memory more. It was here, I am told, that they brought the body of Frederic II., the *Stupor Mundi*, to lie in a place he would have chosen : the man who so nearly made himself an Anti-Christian master of his world : the last of the Emperors to hold, or attempt to hold, the South.

Later they took him on to Palermo, and he lies there now in his porphyry tomb. But Cefalu was nearer to his spirit.

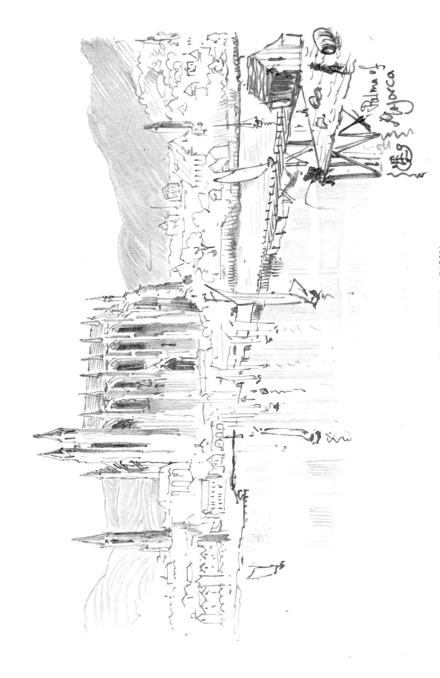

CHAPTER XI

Palma of Majorca

THE PORT AND CATHEDRAL: PALMA.

To face page 87.

PALMA OF MAJORCA

THE reconquered towns are of two kinds. There are those in which the Mohammedan swept over the Roman fabric, submerged it, and either deſtroyed it or transformed it into an Arabian thing ; using, indeed, the ſtones of Rome and preserving a barbaric memory of Roman forms, but wholly changing the spirit of Roman building and leaving its conſtruƈtions ſteeped in the Oriental air ; degraded, also, and much lessened ; with plaster, chipped, taking the place of carven marble ; hovels, the place of houses ; a few Eaſtern and secret palaces, the place of great public buildings ; innumerable coloured detail, the place of simplicity and grandeur. Of this sort are Sousse, and all the ancient towns yet surviving between Tunis and the Atlantic.

The other half of them are the ruined skeletons of Roman things like Timgad or Volubilis.

These, the African cities, a modern conqueſt has violently affeƈted. Some it has turned into French cities like Algiers ; some, like Tunis, it has half changed ; but everywhere the influence

of Islam has strongly survived. The second sort
is made up of those forms of which the recovery
came quite early, during the Dark, or very early
Middle Ages, before the Saracen had had time to
take root fully, and while the conflict between the
great Arabian heresy and Western Christendom
was still a war of life and death—as it may be
again. Of this kind is Cefalu, in Sicily, of which
I have just written, and of this kind are Leon and
Huesca and Burgos and in general the towns of
northern Spain; if we exclude Saragossa, which
stood out much longer than the rest, through the
skilful alliances and concessions of its Emirs. In
these towns Christendom came back with violence; all, or nearly all, the relics of the Eastern
alien were wiped out, and everything was remade
in Western fashion.

Palma of Majorca is a bridge between these two
kinds. It was recovered long after the tide had
turned, and in a generation long familiar with
Eastern things. Toledo had been firmly held
for two long lifetimes. The whole epic of the
three first Crusades had been worked out, and
Jerusalem taken and lost again, after a hundred
years. The crisis of the Albigensian peril—in
which the northern French expelled an Asiatic
horror from the south—had passed; the decisive
battle of Navas de Tolosa had already given back
the great bulk of the Peninsula to our culture;
the decisive battle of Muret had already saved our

PALMA OF MAJORCA : TOWER SHOWING ISLAMIC INFLUENCE.

To face page 88.

religion. The high medieval civilisation (of which that thirteenth century was the flower) was in its full vigour—when the fleet sailed out from Catalonia in 1229 for the reconquest of the Balearic Islands.

A very young man, James of Aragon, a King in his twentieth year, led them; a crowd of vessels, with 20,000 armed men aboard, 4000 of them knights. On the last day of the year, Palma was stormed, and within twelve months the last Moorish remnant in the mountains had surrendered.

The restoration of an European city in the place of a Mohammedan pirate port began at once. The emir's great house became the king's palace : on its garden terrace, boldly above and against the shore which looks to Africa, was immediately founded that astonishing cathedral of which, as one comes in from the south overseas, one can not say at first whether it is a church or a fortress ; which is, and was built for, a challenge. On the western hill which dominates the harbour, the city and the bay, the castle of Bellver rose—feudal : a cousin to all the others of France and Spain and the Holy Land : to Château Gaillard as to Kerak, or Conway. In the streets of the town the mosques disappeared, stone Christian houses replaced the packed, white-washed hives of Barbary, and open markets the strange dark tunnels of Eastern merchandise.

Yet something of that long Islamic past remained. You will not find that past in a skyline or in a horse-shoe arch, nor even in details—save in one place, the little Moorish baths which still stand, half ruinous in a lovely garden. But an effect of Barbary is on the place. The tower of St. Cean is modern enough—of the last few centuries, I suppose ; yet at no great distance you might take it for a minaret. The main houses have the great inner courtyard which the Mohammedans had themselves inherited from Rome, and they turn their life inwards after the Eastern fashion, not outwards to the street.

These open inner courts of the houses of Palma are a special mark of the town : they have a character of their own, quite distinct, which does not recall Cordova or Seville, though there, also, this influence of North Africa is present. The line which stamps them is that of the very broad and flattened arch supported on short pillars, simple in capital and base. Everywhere you find that same form, and nowhere is it more striking than when it is combined, in the greatest of the old merchant palaces, with broad, noble staircases behind, half open to the court and covered by great roofs of dark wood, carved over all their surface and supported upon figured beams. Their number is as remarkable as is their individuality. I know not how many there may be, but scores, certainly, and perhaps, small and great,

more than a hundred of these *patios*, all in the
same spirit of grandeur and fulness, all recalling
the merchant wealth of so central a point in
the western Mediterranean, and all indefinably
touched with something of the eastern past, far
less than Africa, but more than Sicily.

Only the cathedral shows nothing of this slight,
permanent Moorish tradition, though it stands
side by side with the Islamic Palace, the old court
of the Emirate. It is wholly of Europe; even
more northern than its peers in the other great
Sees of Spain. For though it is cubic and of
great breadth for its height—which is the Iberian
tradition in shrines—yet it is not a cavern of
darkness like Barcelona or Tarragona, and it even
lacks that enclosed choir, blocking the centre of
the nave, which, in continental Spain, is universal;
the high altar is in full view of every part, and
what is chanted there is heard resonant, but without echo, everywhere.

The fortress-character of the cathedral, of which
I have spoken, is most evident from the sea. It
is on the seaward, southern side of the large building that enormous stone buttresses arise, so plain,
so wide, so square-hewn that they suggest a high
castle wall of prodigious thickness rather than a
temple. They were intended to give that effect.
They were set up as a symbol against the corsairs
from the coast beyond, only a day's fair sail away,
who continued right into our own time—till the

twenties of the nineteenth century—to harry those seas ; coming chiefly from Algiers. In connection with which cutthroats, how many people know that as late as Charles II.'s reign the Algerine sea-robbers ran up north as far as the mouth of the channel, showed the lateen sails and the long banks of rowers in the Irish seas, and gave the call to prayer over Cork harbour ?

A modern restoration, ill-conceived and modelled on Burgos, has spoiled the west end of this great church ; but the rest is triumphant. It is the building in which can best be seized the struggle for the recapture of the Mediterranean. Looking at its northern wall from the sea (as the Algerian pirates saw it when they hovered round the coasts their people had lost) one might wonder what light, or if any light, reached to the nave within. It looks like one mass of unbroken stone, flanked with square towers in which no solution is apparent. It is all strength. There is only one other thing to compare with it, and that is the solid fragment of Narbonne which reproduces the same effect of sheer (and blank) mass, resisting attack and immovable under it.

The Moorish bath, in its tiny scale, its darkness, its imperfection and weakness of execution, its use of old Roman material, its isolation—all it has—is characteristic of the thing which the young Conqueror who re-established us in the Balearics set out to destroy.

The tiny arches are supported upon shafts which the Roman order had left behind it, but these columns had been picked up in the ruins, for they are set up at random, without choice—one of them upside down! Upon the summit of each the Oriental has attempted some faint memory of the Corinthian capital. He has rudely carved half-a-score of rough knobs, which barely hint at the old acanthus-leaves, and he had some memory of the central moulding in the abacus—but he only hinted at it. The arch of small brick above—Roman also in tradition—he pinched at the base into that re-entering curve which is, in our eyes, the special mark of Mohammedan building, but which will, I think, like the dome and the minaret, be found to derive from Byzantium. For Islam creates nothing.

And now, what will another lifetime do to Palma? It is not a century since George Sand brought Chopin here to Majorca, and killed him by the experiment. The island was unknown; it was a daring journey. Steam and still more the modern chaos in things of the mind began, twenty years later, to destroy what they could of proportion, personality and beauty here as everywhere. I have heard for these thirty years past that the special soul of Palma can not survive, that it is with every day more visited and becoming from a thing, a name. I expected when I revisited it to find it half ruined. I was not so.

Twenty-one years and more had passed since I had laſt sailed into that bay from the Barbary coaſt, and seen the square rock of the cathedral under the dusk of a winter dawn. In that long space of time Palma has loſt less than any other of the towns I know.

I think it will endure. It has the Catalonian tenacity and vigour in its blood, and it should resiſt decay. It is to be hoped that it will, and it is even to be prayed for ; there are not many cities left in which tradition is alive and beauty preserved without effort, without archaism, without affeſtation ; but as part of a continued life.

CHAPTER XII

SOUSSE, WHICH IS HADRUMETUM

A HUNDRED miles or so south of Carthage Bay, on the now bare and scorched shore which faces the Levanter, stands Sousse.

If Cefalu is the type of an antique town, pre-historic, then Punic, then Greek, then under Roman rule, then swamped by Islam, but so early recovered by our race that the whole trace of the Orient has been wiped out of it, Sousse is the best type of the other extreme : prehistoric, then Punic, then Græco-Roman—but so changed by Islam that it has lost its ancient body and soul, and is wholly turned Mohammedan to the eye and mind. Palma of Majorca, as I have said, is the link between the two types of the recovered towns.

Sousse has lost everything, down to its very name ; yet it was a port ; Punic in origin, and Tyrian, therefore, for centuries—perhaps for nearly a thousand years. It was next Græco-Roman, and after the brief Vandal misrule con-tinued to be Græco-Roman until the Arab cavalcade overwhelmed it more than twelve centuries ago. But once that shock had been delivered its transformation and degradation

began, and, so far as it is possible to destroy the
strong things of Pagan and Christian antiquity,
here they were destroyed.

The Crusades failed to affect the town; Europe
never recovered its foothold until our own time,
quite lately; and when Europe came back two-
thirds of the town area and the great old port of
the ancients, the chief haven of all that coast after
Carthage, had disappeared. Nothing remained
but a miserable square of Saracenic tunnel
markets, low, rough, whitewashed domes, and
little cubes of huts or houses, with here and there
the rough, lime-splashed tower of a minaret, and
round it all the patched, degraded walls of what
had once been a Roman City. The surrounding
country lost its impress of Rome. The marble
was looted and broken, the columns fell. In the
place of temple and statue and arch you have the
Eastern village suburb in its groves.

For Sousse was *Hadrumetum*, and in its harbour
and outside its triple line of defence was played
the first act of a great drama among the stories of
the world; the final triumph of Cæsar. No one
to-day could guess that ever Sousse had had such
dignity of name and function; so thoroughly
does Islam ruin what it has occupied.

But Hadrumetum had played a great part long
before Cæsar. Hannibal, at the end of the second
Punic War, fighting that last despairing fight upon
the soil of his own country, made it his base. In

96

THE WALLS OF SOUSSE.

To face page 96.

the third Punic War it deserted Carthage, and was rewarded by its new Roman masters with a local freedom. They loaded it with wealth and made it greater than ever it had been before, building three great ports with a breakwater of half-a-mile to shelter them, crowding it with Grecian art and noble, ponderous stone. It became (after Utica, and while Carthage was still in ruins) the second town of Africa. And now it is what you may see, a whitewashed collection of small, barbarous things, shrunk to a third of its old size, or less, and having for a memory of its past nothing but a few stones here and there ; hardly any of them in the city.

All about it, ten miles one way, twenty another, forty another, a hundred another, stand the monumental ruins which still bear witness to the ravaging evil of the Mohammedan tide. But in Sousse nothing. Even those great works of the harbour disappeared, and the French, when they brought Europe back forty years ago to begin the recovery, had to build up a new port from first to last.

I have said that it was here that was played out the first scene in that great drama, the final triumph of Cæsar.

After Pharsalia, the republican leaders had taken refuge in Africa. They had twenty legions. Cæsar from Sicily proposed to take the initiative and to attack. He had with him but one legion,

which grew to no more than five : six hundred
Gallic horsemen, who increased to no more than
two thousand.   His opponents had behind them,
in alliance with them and almost in command
over them, all the forces of the native kingdom
which lay inland behind the coast towns.   Even
this small force of his Cæsar failed to concentrate,
and the story of what followed is very good proof
that fortune has more to do with the greatness of
soldiers even than character.   It was on the
twenty-seventh of December, in the year 707 of
the city, that Cæsar left Sicilian land ; a storm
dispersed his convoys, and when he saw Cape Bon
on the morning of the third day he had with him
not more than two thousand men and a squadron
of his French cavalry.   Nevertheless, in the same
temper which had made him march north in
Gaul, eight years before, after suffering defeat in
Auvergne—the temper of audacity which had
always hitherto befriended him—he determined
to land that small force and risk all upon the
throw, trusting to some favour of heaven (which
he mocked) for the return and concentration of
his remaining ships.

He went on all that day, until, in mid-afternoon,
he stood opposite the triple harbour of Hadrumetum, and could see from his decks the large
town reaching gently upward inland more than
a mile every way, and its suburb, almost as great
as itself, lying off along the shore to the south ;

beyond the centuries-old wall the new Roman additions and the great ditch which bounded all. Within were two legions under Considius. It must have been the superiority of his human material which permitted Cæsar's landing in the face of such a threat, and although to his few score of French horsemen there were opposed within the walls of the city, large bodies of the irregular native cavalry.

He spent the morrow, the last day of the year, in recognising every part of the defence. He saw that assault was out of the question with his small numbers, and on the first of January he marched off south to Monastir, fighting (as he broke contact with the enemy garrison of Hadrumetum) small rear-guard actions, in which the Northern riders had overwhelmingly the better of opponents more than ten times as numerous. This safe escape of Cæsar, this bold landing in the face of odds, and unwounded retirement, was the inception of the campaign which ended in Thapsus.

You would never guess it to-day. To see Sousse as it stands now you would think it had never known the great hour or the nobility of our blood.

Two long days' march to the south there still stands that huge relic and proof of what the ancient civilisation was, the ruined amphitheatre, which the Mohammedans called, and call, El Djem : like a ruined coliseum in the midst of the

sand. In the hill country to the north still stand
the noble temple of Sbitla, the columns of Djebba
and fifty other remaining proofs of what we lost
by that catastrophe of Asiatic invasion. But in
Sousse all I could find of the past were the huge
Punic stones at the base of the wall, a fragment
of a figure, a fragment or two of a column and one
small building from the depths of the Dark Ages,
an old fossil of the ninth century, in which one
can still see how dependent the invader was for
stone and for all permanent work upon the
Roman order which he had destroyed.

For in that little building the pillars supporting
Moorish arches are the last pillars of Grecian art,
and the very lintel of the door is made of a fragment of column set flat. Just as in those Arab
baths of Palma, the new men could not build even
their little dwarf things without the material of
the world which they ruined.

Nevertheless, Sousse-Hadrumetum did remain ; the town was not allowed to die—and
why that was I have often wondered. Perhaps
the presence of some great treasure, well kept in
some strong building of the Acropolis which
became the Kasbah and is to-day the seat of the
French garrison, pinned the Arabs to the place ;
or perhaps that noble harbour, which their
negligence and incapacity allowed to decay into
nothingness, still maintained a trade which Carthage had lost. But, at any rate, these enemies of

SOUSSE : THE ROUGH TOWER OF THE MINARET.

To face page 100.

the Roman name who so thoroughly depopulated Carthage continued to inhabit Sousse, and it has thus held a life uninterrupted for three thousand years; three great and almost equal periods: Punic (with Greek models and influences), Roman, Islamic.

If it were possible to call up the past visibly and to see the successive fates of landscape under those successive waves of religion (which are the determinants of all changes in culture) the roadstead of Sousse assuredly would be the best standpoint to take up in all the Mediterranean area.

First you would see, before the beginning of recorded history, some little group of native Berber huts grouped round a small rocky elbow of the beach which gave a tiny refuge from the Levanter. Next a fleet of merchant vessels from the east coming to trade and settle, and a Phœnician city rising before you, girdled by a wall of great rough stone, its citadel crowned by the temple of some vile Tyrian god, its colour that vivid yellow with which the Semitic culture of all this coast marked its erections. You would see the first little natural refuge expanding into the old and mighty port of Hadrumetum, and from the groves all about it, the very fertile fields, the grey sweeps of olive and the mile-wide stretches of corn, wealth pouring on to those quays for export to other lands; wealth springing up every-

where from that famous plain to the very roots
of the mountains rising miles away inland : a
land still watered and with many trees.

Then you would see a slow transformation in
colour and in form as the centuries drew on toward the moment of the Incarnation and of the
chief revolution in human affairs : the yellow
turning to marble-white ; statues, by the quays,
of a newer and more perfect kind ; the Corinthian
column everywhere and the flat triangle of the
Grecian temple front. It was from such a city
that the last reserves of Hannibal poured out, and
it was such a city that increased for four hundred
years and more, under the universality of the
Empire.

With the misrule of the Vandal Federates you
might have marked some touch of ruin—but not
much : a burned building here and there un-
restored ; a column fallen and not raised again.
But still that same wealth all around ; trees and
the human climate which trees bring and dense
growth for human sustenance in corn and olive
all over the plain to the rocky hills on the
horizon.

That was what Belisarius found and took when
Justinian restored the Empire in Africa and gave
his own name to the city ; that was still what the
first Arab horsemen saw who came swarming in
like locusts from their over-running of Cyrene
and their mastery of Egypt—many squadrons,

KALAA SERHIRA, JUST NORTH OF SOUSSE : A ROMAN SUBURBAN TOWN, TRANSFORMED AND TURNED MOHAMMEDAN.

To face page 102.

clad in large white cloaks and sitting the small, nervous, desert horses.

They conquered, and the evil transformation began. Century after century you would have seen the trees grow less and less, the plain lying baked and naked, more and more burned under the sun, the harbour works crumbling, all the high and noble buildings of the town falling to a baser level, and its area shrinking at the same time, and all the monuments of the days of its greatness ruined and at laſt forgotten.

Now Europe has come back, but with what chance of permanence here? And what new town, if any, will Europe build, worthy of the old and proud widespread Roman city which has disappeared?

CHAPTER XIII

GUELMA

IF one were looking for the moſt typical example of what European civilisation has done upon its return to Africa, one would choose Guelma.

I do not mean by the words ' typical example ' the moſt remarkable, ſtill less the moſt admirable, whether in government or in architecture and other externals. I mean : the place where the new effort shows all its various qualities, good and bad, at their average. There in the little town among the mountains you have the ſtrong memories of the Roman time, the mixture in almoſt equal proportions of the European and the native, the astonishing agricultural development with which French energy has renewed the fertile land of North Africa, the visible relics of the conqueſt, and all this set in one of the fineſt and moſt characteriſtic landscapes of Barbary. For Guelma ſtands upon a rise of land central to a great cup in the mountains, a sort of half-way house between the sea and the ancient capital, Conſtantine.

As you approach the little place, you have the

GUELMA.

To face page 104.

full illusion of Europe; especially if you come upon it in the spring. The beginning of the desert is not three long days' walk away, not half a day in a motor : at least, what I should call the beginning of the desert, which is the foot of Aurès and the famous cleft in the hills which is called in Arabic ' the Mouth of the Sahara.' Yet here, all around Guelma, are nothing but rich crops, green mountain sides, running water, and even, what is rare in Africa, large groups of timber.

What aids the illusion is the great French road running between rows of trees on either side, now mature; a road which might be in the Bourbonnais; which might have been transported bodily across the Mediterranean ! And as one walks along it up the hill, one cannot but expect at the end of it an old French town.

It is when one comes near enough to distinguish detail that the African character is first apparent, for the walls still stand which were built when the whole country was full of fighting, and when the occupation had just begun. And these walls are everywhere loop-holed for defence against attack. In the same view you see, standing up among the group of small provincial houses, essentially French in character, standing up in the neighbourhood of a very French parish church and a typically French market-place (with the unfailing foliage of the

Mail), the minaret of a mosque and the huge semicircle of the Roman theatre ; a pendant to which, upon the other side of the town, is the large ruins of the baths. It stands after two thousand years in the midst of the barracks where the garrison is quartered.

There has been a deliberate effort to restore the memory of Rome, and to impress its greatness upon the men who came in upon its decline, and pillaged its ruins. The portrait statues set up by antiquity, found buried or cast aside, have been raised again upon their pedestals in the public street, and, quite lately, the theatre has been made to look once more as much as possible what it was when Cyprian was the head of the struggling African church, or earlier when the Antonines still ruled the world.

I am not sure whether the French have done well or ill in this restoration. Politically their object was just, and has, perhaps, been obtained ; but to the eye, a thing half of which is modern, and which is yet exactly modelled upon the antique, has something strange about it. Perhaps it is only the effect of the onlooker's age.

When I first saw this mighty thing I was a young man in my thirty-fourth year. It stood then, a huge hollow of very large worn stones, rising in tiers of seats one above the other, with grass growing between, and shrubs, and, perhaps, the half of it in ruins. Where the stage had been

GUELMA : ROMAN THEATRE.

To face page 106.

was then nothing but a level sward; the ground fell abruptly away beyond, and the great cup looked solemnly out towards the mountains north and west. I drew a picture of it in pencil to illustrate the book *Esto Perpetua* which I wrote to describe Africa.

Now, visiting the place after twenty years, I cannot wholly approve the change. Every old stone that could still serve was kept, but all that had fallen into ruin was replaced. An exact scholarship looked after every detail, and has even been at the pains of setting round the half-circle of high exterior wall those sockets in which were placed, so many centuries ago, the masts to support the awning that shaded the audience from the African sun. Indeed, the great theatre of Guelma is actually in use again, and on its new stone stage has been acted the drama of the Ancients and of the Moderns. 'Great' I have called it. Yet, somehow, it seems smaller with its modern reparations and close copying of the past. It seemed more vast and more noble in its abandonment, as it had remained for so many centuries, and as I first saw it all those years ago.

· Guelma is typical not only in its unison of the modern French, the Mohammedan and the Antique, nor only in its chief character of an African market town, serving the new agricultural wealth of the province; it is typical also of that domesticity and lack of magnificence which, so far, has marked the return of Europe to this land. Algiers and Oran are great French cities, and Tunis and the lesser places bear the same stamp. But the ancients raised monuments everywhere, even in the smaller towns, of a character and endurance, of a nobility to the eye, and of a permanence in intention, which our modern civilisation fails to reach. There has been, perhaps, but one modern moment comparable to the many centuries of the pagan civilisation in the magnificence of its building, and that was the time of Louis XIV. The spirit did not last; it fell from grandeur to prettiness, and after that, save for the brief classical interlude of the end of the First Republic and of the Empire, nothing worthy has appeared.

And Guelma shows all this. There is nothing further that Europe has done, even on a small scale, to compare with the baths in their ruin, or the theatre—let alone with what the whole place must have been when those buildings were alive. The Guelma of antiquity was no larger than the Guelma of to-day. It served the same social purpose, a market town for the farmers in the highlands and of the rich seaward valleys of the Tell. But even in a place upon so small a scale Rome and Greece were able to impose the stamp of nobility. We to-day neither desire to impose such a mark nor are we able to do so.

But with this lack of magnificence goes that pleasant stability of small fortune that you find even better rooted here in Africa than in the mother country, and it applies not only to the colonists, but to the native people. The new civilisation has not only created a new agriculture for its own people, it has multiplied—I know not by how much, but very largely—the wealth of the original Mohammedan farmers. Yet even to-day it is curious to note how the native African race clings to its traditional culture of the soil; with what suspicion or indifference it looks upon agricultural machinery; and what a contrast it continues to make with the increasing area of European tilling.

Yet change is taking place. The occasion of my last passing through Guelma was a sort of little local exhibition or fair of agricultural machinery. And of the many buyers a large minority was native. It was strange to note the big American advertisements attracting a crowd of turbaned men mixed with European farmers, and to see pictures of a reaper and binder on the lands of the Middle West stuck up here in the African hills for an advertisement in that half-Eastern, half-European scene.

Africa is full of such things—I mean full of such odd contrasts and mixtures, and I, for my part, find therein the chief pleasure of African travel. But nowhere did I see contrasts more

numerous and balanced than in Guelma that day
of the fair. American industry, Islam, the eternal
Gallic peasant—and the majesty of Rome, a visible
ghost, a background for it all.

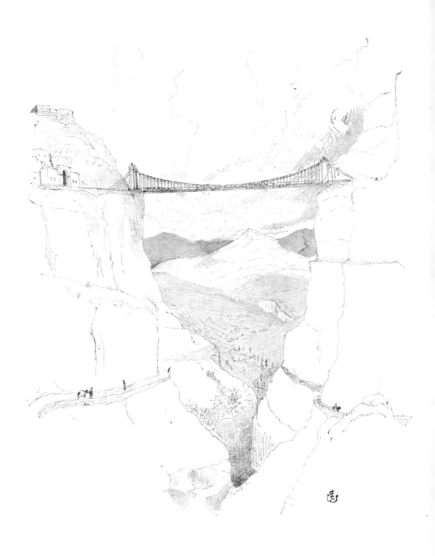

CONSTANTINE : MOUTH OF THE RUMMEL GORGE.

To face page 111.

CHAPTER XIV

CONSTANTINE

CONSTANTINE is, perhaps, the most deeply stamped city of the West. It is certainly the one which, in site and relief, stands out most strongly of all those that I have seen between the Russian plains and the Atlantic.

Many towns have one great hill or rock to mark them, for most towns have risen round the nucleus of a stronghold; and an isolated rock, if only it has water, is the best choice for early defence. Many towns are peninsular in shape; built on a loop of river and only to be approached by a narrow neck of land. Such are Angoulême, Luxemburg, Poitiers; and many of these peninsular towns have something of a cliff or steep bank defending them for some part of their circuit.

But Constantine is like nothing else on earth that ever I saw. And from the first moment that I saw it, it has stood vividly fixed in my mind, as, I suppose, it will stand in the mind of any man who comes upon it from any side.

For the note of Constantine is this: that it is a considerable city, standing quite alone, upon a platform wholly isolated save for the narrowest isthmus-neck of approach. On every side beyond that very narrow neck of approach there fall away from its walls not steep or common cliffs, but tremendous precipices. It is, as it were, one rock as big as a mountain ; but a mountain sufficiently levelled upon its upper side against the sky to give foundation for a large town. Fifty or sixty thousand human beings may have lived crowded upon that strange table. Upon the one side the prodigious overhanging rocks look down on a broad valley, I know not how many hundred feet below ; upon the other, they plunge into, and equally overhang, a gorge so deep that when you look down into it you think you have seen the river bed at the bottom, when really you have only caught sight of a ledge and a track running half-way between the height and the stream. That stream is the tumbling, yellow torrent which has been called since the Mohammedan conquest ' El Rhummel,' that is, ' The Tawny ' ; and I think it will give some conception of the gorge and of its depth when I say that the noise of its waters, even in spate, are hardly heard in the night by a man upon the city walls so high above them.

Segovia is of this character—a town on a rock, and so is Castro Giovanni. But neither of them can compare for magnitude of impression with Constantine.

THE FONDUK OR STABLE, WITH MOSQUE BEYOND THE GORGE.

To face page 112.

The neck, or isthmus, by which the plateau of Constantine is reached, is much narrower than in the parallel instances of the other, similar towns. The rocks which bound Constantine's almost isolated plateau are everywhere more precipitous and the plunge to the water-level more profound; and the approach also rises steeply, and the keep of the stronghold, the Kasbah, the Castle, is on the frontier point of it. The prow of that ship rises in a high forecastle, the poop is low.

Enemies storming Constantine have not only had for so many centuries to approach by a very narrow pass; but having once mastered that unique neck of land, they had the task imposed upon them of still fighting uphill all the way, till they came to the last fortification—the heart of the place—at the very extreme of the lifting plateau.

Nevertheless, Constantine (like nearly all these seemingly impregnable places) has been stormed time after time. Indeed, the cities that have boasted many centuries of immunity, or even complete immunity, from conquest, have never been cities apparently inexpugnable. Cities which seem made for eternal defence, these, by the very fact of their challenge, lure armies on : and Constantine, which still looks to the eye all but impregnable, has fallen with every new conquest of Barbary ; the last not a century ago ; the next to be we know not when.

The city was originally called Cirta—a word which some men think means ' the Rock ' in a Punic dialeﬅ. And Cirta it remained up to the conversion of the Weﬅ from paganism 1600 years ago, and in popular speech long after that. But the official name was changed by the great Conﬅantine when he had conquered the world with his French and English forces againﬅ the Southern and Levantine troops of his pagan rivals ; and the new name had so far taken root when the Mohammedan desert men came swarming over all this land that they kept it in a corrupted form, and that its inhabitants call it ' Ksantina ' to this day. Nevertheless, I know not why, it is always as Cirta that it returns to my mind ; perhaps because one sees the word so often in modern works upon ancient North Africa ; perhaps because that which moﬅ profoundly moved me when I firﬅ saw the place, the old tombs, have that name upon them—coming as they do long before the final revolution which eﬅablished the Catholic faith upon the ruins of the Roman world. Of those old inscriptions above the dead, one ﬅill haunts me. I put it into my writing upon North Africa many years ago. It is upon the tomb of a woodland priestess who died young, and for whom her friends thus wrote upon the ﬅone : ' The Dryads wept.'

It will never be Cirta again officially, for the Punic language is dead. And even the Berber

CONSTANTINE : THE NATIVE QUARTER.

To face page 114.

language, from which, perhaps, the name derived, still older than the Syrian merchants of Carthage, only carries on a painful life, and will not here oust again (one may surely say) the Semitic or the Latin speech. But it was to Cirta that the Kings of the Berbers returned from before the beginning of history to triumph after victory, or to stand a siege after defeat. It was in Cirta that the great tragedy of Jugurtha was accomplished. It was back to Cirta that the host of native cavalry retired, when Cæsar threatened to achieve, and achieved, his final victory, near the Tunisian shore.

If there is one place in which I could regret the recovery to Roman land and the return of Europe to North Africa (which is justly but a province to Europe) that place is Cirta : Constantine. For it seems to have a sort of savage right to independence, and its tremendous cliffs challenge order and the domination of universal government. It is a great chieftain's town.

The birds of the air are not yet accustomed to think that Constantine is a human capital, though it has been so now for longer than any man can remember. The vultures love to poise in mid-heaven above the abysses around the city, flying on a level with its highest roofs ; and I have known days when, the mist covering the lower ground of the broad valleys to the left and of the gorge to the right, all Constantine seemed like a thing of the air ; a city setting out to navigate between earth and sky.

The French have done with such a site what might be predicted of their energy, their bureaucracy, their order ; also their itch for change. Upon that narrow neck of approach which the Roman, the Arab, the Turk, the Vandal, the Byzantine generals had forced in turn, they have put up their monument to the great Lamoricière —but I very much prefer his noble tomb in Nantes, although it be but a translation from the Italian. Upon the pedestal of this statue they have the words of the trooper who shouted to his general through the dusk after the first repulse, on the eve of victory : ' To-morrow the town will be yours, or I shall be dead.' The French have also put up a statue of Constantine himself, the August, the Victorious. He is just outside the railway station on the far side of the town, on the edge of the gorge whence you look across the deep to the ramparts of the city. But the most characteristic thing they have done is to emphasise this unique isolation and dominance and height in two ways : first by building flying bridges which span the gulf and show its dizziness, next by driving a road of the most fantastic sort all round the circuit of those unclimbable rocks. It should not be so, perhaps, but so it is, that this new highway, cut into the precipice (in some places driven in tunnels and arches through huge

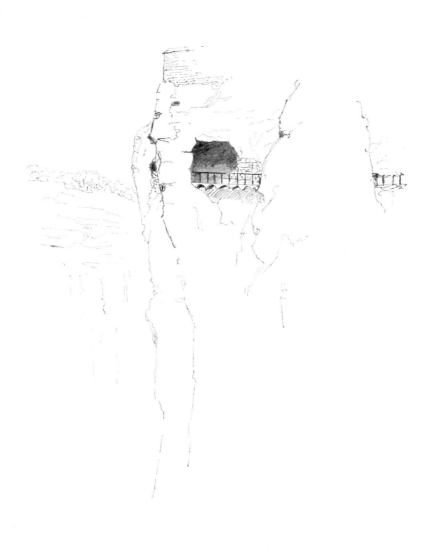

CONSTANTINE : CORBELLED AND TUNNELLED ROAD.

To face page 116.

boulders, and in other places so poised that from its parapet you look sheer down into the gorge) does not detract from the fearfulness of the place, nor even from its majesty. It enhances both.

I have, in speaking of other parts of Barbary, asked the question: What will happen? Can it endure? But of Constantine, on the rock of Cirta, I have little doubt. These things are greater than man, and even should man abandon them, it will stand as mighty as ever. What a stone!

CHAPTER XV

CHERCHELL, WHICH IS CÆSAREA

I HAVE heard all my life that if you find a good thing you should keep it to yourself, and I have heard that piece of advice particularly emphasised in the matter of places. I have found it to be false. Other people do not believe you when you sing the praises of a place, or if they believe you they do not take the trouble to follow in your footsteps. Or if they do, they are of that kind which is worthy of the place and does not spoil it. At any rate, I will praise Cherchell. I did not know that in this strange land of Africa, with its meeting of burning desert and snow, its high lands and its too biting sun, there could be so charming, so secluded, so recollected a corner of foliage and sea.

From the first time I saw it years ago (and I did not on that occasion go into the town itself) until my visit of the other day, the memory of that coast has remained with me. When you get out of the suburbs of Algiers (less sordid on this eastern side than are commonly the suburbs of a great town) you follow the road along the coast, having upon your left the hills of the coast

The Trees & Roman Harbour of Cherchell.

THE TREES AND ROMAN HARBOUR OF CHERCHELL.

To face page 118.

range and upon your right the shining of the Mediterranean.

It is a belt of great wealth ; its habitations dotted here and there, few villages and no towns ; the road excellent and well served. Some half-way along it there rises upon your left on one of the hills that huge mausoleum of which no man knows the origin, but which may well be the tomb of the Numidian kings before the Romans came. The Arabs call it by a strange name : ' The Tomb of the Christian Woman.' As you reach its neighbourhood there rises up before you, projecting into the sea, a mountain which had upon either side of it two very ancient and famous towns, Tipasa and Cæsarea, both of them great merchant towns, with harbours built by the Romans, each of them playing its great part in history ; each of them wholly extinguished through the irruption of the Mohammedan con-quest ; each of them re-erected as modern, carefully laid-out, large villages rather than towns, after the re-entry of Europe during the last eighty years.

Of the two Cæsarea (the name of which has changed into Cherchell) is the more remarkable. It is here that the last of the half-Nubian kings built his court, with that queen of his who was called ' The Moon,' Selene. She was the daughter of Antony and Cleopatra.

In its great days the town covered a mile on

every side. Its walls ran up almost to the summit
of the hills and down to the sea-coast, to the east
and west of the great haven ; it was a white mass
of porticoes and noble courts, temples, colonnades, statues and palaces of marble ; the chief
town of Africa, and loaded with all that the
revenue of a nation could purchase from the
artists of the Eastern Sea, from the Greeks of
the Islands and of Egypt. One cannot approach
a site of that kind without some movement of the
heart.

The last of the way lies through a broad and
very fertile valley, with that high seaward mountain looking down upon it from the east, and
with another high line of peaks enclosing it upon
the west. The valley floor is a garden of vines
and wheat and olive, and the great French road
goes through it, ruled straight after the French
fashion, and with its avenue of trees on either
side. But until one is quite close to Cherchell
there is no sign of the place, for it lies hidden
behind a lesser promontory round which the road
turns, immediately before entering the western
gate of the place.

The first sign that one is coming to what was
the capital of all that wealthy land is the high ruin
of a gateway which a man with the same name as
my own (I was pleased to see !) had put up, something less than two thousand years ago, to be the
monument of his wealth and an introduction to

CHERCHELL: ROMAN THEATRE, MOORISH BATHS AND CHRISTIAN CHURCH.

To face page 120.

CHERCHELL : THE AQUEDUCT.

To face page 120.

his country house. The villa has gone for ever and its mansion ; but this gateway remains with its inscription. Next, as one comes still nearer Cherchell there appear upon the left of the hills the ruined arches of the great aqueduct which nourished the town. Lastly, one turns sharply round the corner of a low promontory and one sees the simple modern houses of the place and some trees in the field outside the walls.

The natural charm of it lies in that marriage of trees with salt water, which is so rare in landscape, and which, when one can find it, has an effect like nothing else ; perhaps from its strangeness. Everywhere in and near Cherchell you look down upon the sea through a vista of trees. The *Mail*, or French Central place, of the village is a deep grove of trees which look astonishingly old, seeing that the French could not have planted them more than a long lifetime ago. They are gnarled thick trunks of the Bellombra, and you look through, under their branches, at the sea beyond—as you might look through the columns of a temple with doors wide open at the end. When you go through this grove and come at the end to the edge of the steep overlooking the harbour—where everything is neat, orderly and clean (for Cherchell is a little model of what such places should be)—and when you look down on the transparent water below, you see sundry stones drowned therein, outside the port ; in the shape of one of these, at least, I thought to recognise a column rolled down from some temple or portico. But what was more remarkable was a long, darkish line standing out from the shore, and this when I had carefully noted it, I found to be the foundation of the great breakwater which antiquity had built for the harbour of so packed and wealthy a city. The modern harbour is but a fraction of what that great haven was, and it is strange to consider how completely so much greatness has disappeared, and to note the hint of it in that dark line—out seawards.

Here, as everywhere, the French have set themselves to impress upon Africa the memory of its high Roman past and to call back the dead to life.

The ruins of the theatre they have not, indeed, restored as they have restored those of Guelma ; but they have disembarrassed the ruins of the rubbish which covered them, and they have displayed the monument to the passer-by. There can one stand, upon the square stones of the highest circle, and comprise in the same glance Rome and Islam. Right opposite the line of the stage the Arab baths mark their violent contrast with the Corinthian columns.

It is so throughout the little town. The columns have been set up again upon their base (the chief of them in the midst of the market-place), and a whole wealth of portrait busts,

CHERCHELL : THE SINGLE COLUMN AGAINST THE SEA.

To face page 122.

inscriptions, trophies, statues of the gods, has
been collected and is being added to yearly from
the fields around.

What most moved me in this was the fine
mutilated, headless statue of some Emperor, still
standing one-legged to rebuke the decay of the
world which he had ruled. But, indeed, Cherchell is so full of the past that a man might spend
a month there learning more and more of that
silent doom whereby states far nobler and greater
than our own must go to sleep at last, and die in
their sleep.

I trust that I may return to Cherchell and fulfil
that mood, looking from its vineyards, through
its groves, down to its unchanging sea.

CHAPTER XVI

TIMGAD AND VOLUBILIS: THE OUTPOSTS OF THE
DESERT

THE dead cities of the Roman Empire are few
in number compared with the survivals;
and the base of all our civilisation was the
city, the town, walled, jealous of its private life,
having its own gods and its own traditions. The
Roman Empire left each city singularly free,
subject only to very general laws; able to preserve what language it had inherited or acquired,
to levy its own local taxes, to make its own legal
regulations. The modern conception of a great
State enforcing uniformity upon all its citizens was
abhorrent to the Roman idea, and that is why
that great reservoir from which all our Streams
descend was universally accepted and formed a
happy and united world-State. Nearly all its
towns have survived. There are few English
towns prior to the industrial revolution which
had not a Roman anceStry; very many of those
which seem to be separate from the old Roman
site in England grew up naturally on its suburbs,
where the land was cheaper and where long
habitation had not brought congeStion and
disease.

But here and there, from various causes, a town died out. Palmyra was swamped by Islam and the desert; even in England where Roman continuity is so marked, Wroxeter and Silchester decayed, we know not how or why—perhaps because the line of travel left them. In Gaul, Alesia has gone, and some half-a-dozen others; Pompeii and Herculaneum are the two most famous which perished in a natural catastrophe, and when one was dug out from its ashes, Pompeii, it retained so many monuments of domestic life that attention has ever since been fixed upon them.

But of the dead Roman towns, two have a special place in my memories of travel, because they were outposts, holding the cause of civilisation against the desert, and casting a challenge, as it were, against the forces which bit into the frontiers of the Empire and at last broke them down.

These two towns which fell into the void, in part through the gaining of the sand, but more through the gaining of the barbarian, are Timgad and Volubilis, the one in Algiers, the other in Morocco. Each stands at the southernmost edge of what the civilised men thought it possible to hold permanently as a city; each overlooks wide spaces of what is now to our Northern eyes desert, and even to the eyes of men native to those climates, burning and arid soil. Each has wholly perished. Each is being restored to the modern eye; the one—Timgad—has reappeared almost in its entirety; the other—Volubilis—is in process of excavation, and we shall shortly have there, as at Timgad, the columns set up again upon their bases, some restoration of the ways, the plan of the whole affair expressed, and its skeleton, so to speak, reconstructed sufficiently for us to imagine what the living thing must have been.

The French, who control both these sites, have been blamed for restoring so much. They have been blamed for exercising this vice or virtue in many other things: in the restoration of their cathedrals and of the pagan remains of antiquity in France itself. Thus I suppose that half the outer stones of Laon are new. Carcassonne is a modern reconstruction of an ancient thing. The rediscovered lower courses of the amphitheatre of Paris are nearly all faced with new stone—and so on. The excuse of the French in so acting is that but for restoration all would fall into ruin. The criticism of their action lies in this: that the restoration masks the original and deceives the looker-on. Upon the whole, I think the French have the best of the argument; it is better to have a restored, and, therefore, a permanent, witness to tradition, than a meaningless heap of stones; it is better to have the front of Notre Dame in Paris, to which Viollet-le-Duc added all those imitated statues of the Middle Ages, and gargoyles not of the thirteenth century, but from his nineteenth-century workshop, than to have shapeless things. At any rate, the French have restored Timgad, and they are beginning to restore Volubilis.

The first of these—Timgad—lies on the northern slope of that great mountain of Aurès, from the southern shoulder of which one gazes out towards the endlessness of the Sahara. The second stands on an upland shelf within a mile or two of the hill town of the Moors, Mulay Idris, north of Meknez, and gazes also southwards over wastes only a little less desolate under a burning sun, and having, far away to the south, the huge, dull, unbroken line, the monstrous Hogback, of the greater Atlas. Because it is nearer to the sea winds of the Atlantic, the plain over which Volubilis looks is more habitable than that of Timgad. Even far away to the south upon the Atlas there are trees. But to our Northern eyes, although the French are now colonising it, it seems a most inhospitable land, parched and irredeemable. The people of the place think otherwise. It has a civilisation of its own for many a day's journey southward. The famous fountains and shady courts of Fez are not so far away. Within an hour or two by motor you have the very large modern port of Casablanca. But the Romans rightly thought that

127

upon placing their town here they had an outpost and would go no further, for the life lived further south is not natural to our race.

Timgad impresses me more powerfully with the past than any other place I know, much more than Pompeii, more, even, than Silchester, which I visit once a year also to recover in its crumbling city wall and its earthen amphitheatre the roots of our life. In Silchester nothing shows except the broken city wall and that earthen mound. Timgad is all exposed ; there is the theatre, there are the tall columns standing as in the forum of Rome itself ; there are the dolphin-carved marble arms of the seats in the market-place ; there is the Triumphal Arch—a great city, and all quite silent. This silence, which has the effect of a living death haunted by the past, the French have enhanced by conducting water again to its fountain, and you hear the plashing of the stream emphasising that emptiness of silence all about. If a man will wander in Timgad long enough of a spring morning, especially if he come late in the season, when the rare visitors no longer reach the place, he will feel arising in himself two lives, the life of his own time which he knows and which has made him, and the life of that immemorial past. It is a terrible, a dangerous, but a fascinating experience.

In Volubilis the experience is other. You have no feeling of haunting, of death, or of isolation ; there are olive groves about you ; there is scanty grass; the lovely little Moorish town of Mulay Idris lies just beyond the dip close at hand; a mountain not wholly barren, clothed with scrub, stands up behind it against the east. Here the impression is rather one of history and of contrast. Here you see how completely the new religion of Islam flooded and drowned the classical and Christian tradition.

The contrast between the few stones still unearthed at Volubilis and Mohammedan Mulay Idris, close at hand, is the contrast between a Poussin or a David and an arabesque of Toledo. It is the contrast between the superbly simple replica of Inigo Jones which forms the façade of the English School at Rome and the Mosque of Cordova—two worlds wholly distinct; the one that pagan and late Christian world of which we are the children : we live by our return to its noble classic lines ; the other, the fantasy which the Mohammedan developed from the Byzantine. Both these places also have about them a character which I love in many a spot I have visited, I mean the character of isolation. The very power of modern civilisation to carry men too rapidly from place to place in a mechanical fashion has left more isolated than ever any place just off the main lines. Of all those who go down to Biskra by the railway from Constantine, or who motor down to that desert oasis by the great French military road, how many have turned those short twenty miles aside to steep themselves in Timgad? And of such few as are beginning to visit Morocco and are grown familiar with Meknez, fewer still make the day's journey northward to Mulay Idris. How many even of these cross the narrow valley to look at what may be to them the meaningless stones of Volubilis? It is a good thing that it should be so. In all my many visits to Silchester I have never found another man gazing at those stones or climbing up the earth of the amphitheatre; and Europe and Barbary are full of such silences. I am glad of it.

CHAPTER XVII

THE HILL OF CARTHAGE

ON a day while spring was still calm upon the Mediterranean and before the great heats had come, I sat in a small simple restaurant, French in management and cooking, half-way up a slope that overlooked the Tunisian Sea. Save for the modest house attached to the place, for one or two villas surrounded by deep gardens, for a small halt (rather than a station) upon a local tramway, there was little habitation around me. One great French road went up the hill behind. No vehicle moved upon it.

In the spring sunlight of that noon the Angelus bell from a church upon the height broke the silence, but for the rest it was an empty place enough, with no hint of the past ; a hillside like any other, not even covered by a village ; a little stopping-place upon a suburban tram line, ten miles from the neighbouring capital.

That hill, that bay, were the Hill and the Bay of Carthage.

Over the ground where I sat at meat the Roman Army roared up in the last moments of the final siege. This quiet, empty slope of deserted ground had been filled with fire and carnage. On the summit where now a private house or two and one new church barely break the empty, rounded height, a vast glory of colonnade and portico massed upward to the dominating chief Temple of Moloch, where the nobility of Carthage made their last resistance and died of their own wills. Before that dreadful day, for half a millennium, the greatest and proudest of human cities had overlooked its ports and stood white and enormous above its wide bay, drawing into itself the fleets of the East and sending out its merchants and its adventurers and its Governors of Empire throughout its world. Nothing remains. The round inner harbours of the city in which those men-of-war were ranked have dwindled to sleepy ponds. The quays and the wharves and the warehouses of a million men have disappeared. There is no noise at all, except the little lap of water upon sand.

Fragments of the great aqueduct are to be found upon the plain, also fragments of the cisterns, fragments of the walls here and there, but nothing apparent. The immense affair has gone for ever, and in its place is nothingness.

There are very many places in the world, no doubt, where something of this emotion is called up and something of the wonder that such great human things can utterly vanish ; but nowhere do I find that lesson impressed as it is impressed upon the site of Carthage; upon that hillside above the sea where Carthage once was.

Hippo, the town of St. Augustine, is striking enough with its poor fragments of ruin remaining alone to testify to its greatness, and its site turned into a mile of vineyard; the bulk of the Numidian Cæsarea of which I have just written, the capital where the daughter of Antony and Cleopatra kept her court, is turned to gardens; and in our own country Silchester of which I have written and Wroxeter fill me deeply with the same sense of mortality, arousing in me the same question as to how the traces of man can so finally leave the earth. But here in Carthage the example is more complete and on a far greater scale.

Here was the second city of the world; a city that was at one time not second, but first. Here lived that great merchant aristocracy which has been compared with our own and with that of Venice. Here stood and functioned that famous polity which Aristotle admired as the best he knew; solid, square, free from turmoil; contemptuously certain of mastery by sea, apparently immune from disaster, and taking its own good fortune for granted.

It has gone altogether. No man to-day can even muse within its ruins as he can muse within the ruins of Timgad or Volubilis. There has been a complete clearance, an uprooting, a visible death. It is amazing.

I have read somewhere that negative things cannot impress the mind; that mere absence, a mere void leaves no stamp upon the memory. I may have thought so before I first stood (so many years ago!) upon the lift of the Byrsa, on the slight slope of what had been the citadel of so famous a state. But since that date I have always known that the death of things can be impressive as the death of men. The other day when I came back to Carthage after so long a space my earlier feeling was redoubled.

This then is the end of what men do upon the surface of the earth during their little passage through the daylight!

The mighty city, I suppose, had its great musicians, and its poets. It bred its great soldiers. One of them ranks with the greatest captains of time. It felt itself necessarily eternal. It has vanished altogether.

I have marvelled often enough how the thing could physically be done. Is it the perpetual work of the earth covering old stones, or the quarrying of men, or what, that obliterates such mighty cities? At any rate they disappear.

I concluded as I returned that night from Carthage through the evening that our ignorance of the past is an abyss.

We do not know how human culture began; for the fullest expression of it in the most enduring material may, it would seem, be dissipated like smoke. We know, of course, that all the argument upon prehistory and the rest is guess-work and all the violent assertion made by popular writers upon it is merely charlatan. But there is more than that. There arises from the contemplation of Carthage hill a conviction that any state may be lost with all its records. We know not what or how many may not have sunk in the profundity of time and perished altogether. We know not how far back stretch the gorgeous cities and the full pageant of culture.

It is with the race as with the individual member of the race. We come out of a darkness which we cannot pierce. We are for a moment in the light. And of what is to come we know nothing.

Part IV
France

CHAPTER XVIII

THE MONUMENTS OF THE RHONE

I WILL not leave the Recovered Cities without a word upon that other shore which the Mohammedan raided but never held. For it is a corner of Europe where the public monuments of antiquity bear witness more than in any other place to the Roman foundations of Europe. I mean the triangle including either side of the lower Rhone between Avignon and the Delta, within which triangle lie the great Roman towns of Nîmes, Avignon and the most ancient town of Arles, and the great Roman viaduct over the Gard River which brought the water to Nîmes, and is one of the noblest structures in Europe. The particular character of this small district of the world, its strong, permanent impress of antiquity and its 'carrying on' (that is, its continuity almost unmixed with the disturbance of outer things), are due to several causes combined.

First, this district was fertile and sheltered. There is a ring of mountains east, north and west which make a wall for it. Next, it was the first expansion of Italy in her Roman experiment of Empire : the large accumulated capital and the

139

ſtrong social habits of Roman society at its height ſtruck roots here as they did elsewhere outside Italy in the Weſt ; but, unlike Italy, the country was not ravaged by the perpetual marching and counter-marching of armies.

It had its share of wars at the end of the Empire and the beginning of the Dark Ages, but much less than had Italy. On the other hand, it did not present that vaſt accumulation of movable wealth which the Italian towns did, from Rome downwards, so that there was less temptation for loot and deſtruction. Laſtly, it was not so perpetually modelled and remodelled by the ceaseless travel and pilgrimage, adminiſtration, missionary effort and legal appeal, such as made all the great roads upon either side of the Apennines, over the passes of the Alps, a stream of men going back and forth for more than one thousand years. Here in this more or less sheltered corner, the old civilisation, based upon the olive and the vine and wheat, found all three, as in Italy. To the north, the olive was lacking. In Italy, perpetual war and perpetual travel confused the record. But here in the Rhone valley and to the eaſt of it, antiquity could eſtablish its memorial. That is why you are more in touch with the end of the Empire and its transformation during the Dark and the Middle Ages, at Arles, at Avignon, at Nîmes than you can be anywhere else in the world.

AVIGNON : THE BRIDGE.

To face page 140.

Of this character Arles bears the deepest imprint. It was, I suppose, the earliest harbour of the Rhone, far away beyond history, before the silting up of the mouth had forbidden the use of the haven. To-day all that activity has transferred to distant Marseilles. But Arles seems to have been the original port, for here you have, in the last stratum, the barbaric implements of men who could not yet use metal, then, in succeeding layers, the proof of habitation by an increasing culture which never dies. Here you have the great theatre of the Imperial time, and the walls of the Dark Ages, and here you see the round Roman arch changed into the pointed, with the advent of the Middle Ages, and here you can follow the column very slowly transformed from its classic to its mediæval form.

Avignon makes a different appeal. Its greatness is late and political. Men certainly held that strong, isolated rock, which is now crowned by the modern pillar and statue of Our Lady and with the careful little garden at her feet, since first these lands were inhabited. It was an obvious stronghold, obviously supplied by the river ; but what made Avignon the great example of the Middle Ages in stone was the transference thither of the seat of the Papacy under the armed force of the French, six hundred years ago ; one of those violent, not permanent, experiments in imposing their power which the French love to

141

attempt and have not ceased to play with since they were a nation. The transference of the Papacy to Avignon came juſt at the moment when the Papal court was widely extending its funƈtions, and, therefore, its revenue, and you had packed into this little area within the city walls that yet ſtand (aſtonished at their reſtored neatness), more wealth than was to be found even in the City of London or in the Island of Paris or in St. James of Compoſtella. As I said of Salamanca, there are no more intereſting places in the world than those in which wealth has been concentrated in the paſt, having since abandoned them. For there you may see the higheſt effort in ſtone of some paſt time, cryſtallised and made permanent, with no modern effort to diſturb it. Of this concentration of money, which went on for a good long lifetime, the monument is the Palace of the Popes. Nothing can convey the effeƈt of that mountain of masonry, save a physical presence under its cliffs of sawn free-ſtone.

We all know that the effeƈt of height or diſtance is one not of scale but of proportion : that Beauvais, for instance, soars higher to the eye than the Eiffel tower and that Old St. Paul's looked much longer than St. Peter's ; but no-where will you find this effeƈt of mass better than you will find it in the Palace of the Popes at Avignon, though I suppose the aƈtual height is

Emma S. Dwane

Avignon Palai des Papes

AVIGNON : PALAIS DES PAPES.

To face page 142.

not greater than that of many office buildings of
to-day, nor the ground plan larger than that of
some average great railway station.

At Nîmes, unlike Arles and still more unlike
Avignon, the effect is one of antiquity, exactly
preserved. There is there little effect of transition. The town is of modern times, with some
additional dignity of the eighteenth century, but
there stand embedded in it, sharply contrasting
with all around, and challenging every lesser later
thing, the scale and proportion of classical effort ;
the proportion, in that lovely little temple which
they call the ' Maison Carrée ' ; the scale, in the
amphitheatre. I suppose all the remaining great
amphitheatres of the Empire, seeing that they
were built upon one plan, should by rights produce one effect upon the mind, or at any rate
effects proportionate to the size of each : El Djem
in the sands of Tunis, Verona, Pola, the Coliseum.
But it is not so. Each has its own spirit—an
illusion, no doubt, but very vivid, and this of
Nîmes dominates the town more than does that
of Verona or of Pola, and far more, also, than
does the far larger Coliseum affect the immensity
of the city of Rome.

But of all the monuments which antiquity has
left to mark this particular countryside of Europe,
the most impressive, the most permanently
enormous in the memory of those who have seen
it is the Pont du Gard. It was late in my life

143

that I first came upon this giant thing, round the corner of the road in the gorge of that lonely valley, spanning the ravine from escarpment to escarpment above the trees. I have often heard of the effect it produced. I could not believe it ; for, after all, it was but a specimen of the round arch, of the regular Roman courses : a simple process of building in tiers from side to side of a ravine. But when one sees the thing, all that is said of it comes true. Its isolation, its dignity, its weight, are all three awful. It looks as though it had been built long before all record by beings greater than ourselves, and were intended to stand long after the dissolution of our petty race. One can repose in it. I confess to a great reluctance to praise what has been praised too much ; but so it is. A man, suffering from the unrest of our time, might do worse than camp out for three days, fishing and bathing under the shadow of the Pont du Gard.

ROCAMADOUR.

To face page 145.

CHAPTER XIX

ROCAMADOUR

O F all that strange limestone country which forms the southern part of the central French mountain group I suppose the best known point is Rocamadour, yet travel does not reach it very largely even now, and probably such travellers as do go to it carry away with them the impression that it is unique. For the railway or the car takes them for the most part to other lands immediately, and few of them indeed go northward and eastward up into that high, half-desert country with its deep cañons and ancient mountain towns.

Yet Rocamadour is only one of perhaps half-a-hundred examples of the way in which man, for innumerable centuries, has used the physical character of the upper Dordogne basin ; and if you wander about that part of the world on foot —which is much the best way—you will carry away the impression of one village and castle and shrine after another, clinging to precipitous crags which overhang the waters in every valley.

To go down the Dordogne itself and make any excursion to right or left is a sufficient experience,

and from such a position Rocamadour is only a
few miles up a lateral valley to the south ; but,
as I shall say, it is not the best way.   Originally
Rocamadour—in historical times at least—was
not a fortress but a shrine.   As a fortress it would
have had no very great value, for, sheerly precipitous as it is on the western side, the approach
from the east is over an open plain without
defensive value.   In other words, Rocamadour
is nothing but the jutting cape of a cliff ; but the
fact that it began as a shrine has made it what it is.
The fact that the shrine was half-way up the
precipice, beginning presumably as a hermitage,
roughly sheltered by the overhanging rock, compelled the building of inns for pilgrims, and the
establishment of shops for providing their necessi-
ties, and all that goes with them.   They were
compelled to choose the very boulders of the cliff
face, clinging to them precariously, having steep
steps for their village ways, and for their only
street one very narrow levelled edge of mountain
road, perhaps a third of the way up the steep.

It is this display of miniature miracles in construction and primitive engineering on a cliff face
which lends all its character to the famous village
—for village it now is, though in the Middle Ages
it must rather have been a small town during the
height of its fame.

The shrine is dedicated to Our Lady and has
been so as far back as we can go ; but a legend,

ROCAMADOUR: ROLAND'S SWORD AND ST. ANTHONY'S CHEST (BY
TRADITION), ON THE TERRACED PLATFORM OF THE SHRINE.

To face page 146.

historically unsupported, gives it an origin either earlier or later than the true one. As the legend runs, the Zaccheus of the Gospels wandered here after persecution in Palestine and built his hermitage half-way up the sheer side of the rock. The certain truth is, that you find a shrine widely visited, and with the name of St. Amadour attached to it, just as the Dark Ages break into the light of the Middle Ages at the time of the Crusades, and that its origin is then already lost in an immense antiquity. It is possible that this antiquity stretches back for years beyond the beginnings of our civilisation—or that of Rome. The heart of the shrine is a subterranean chapel— as at Chartres, and as at the Souterraine, some days away to the north ; and we know how, all over Europe, the shrines of pagan antiquity were taken on by Christendom. Although we have the name, Amadour, it tells us nothing. A vague guess has been made that it corresponds with a real historical personage, St. Amator, but of this there is no proof. It is to me half the fascination of Rocamadour that it goes back to the beginning of things—and beyond.

It is one of the places in Europe whose name has been revived, and such a thing is always pleasant to discover. An endless stream of pilgrims, kings, saints—among them was St. Dominic, came to give thanks long after for the victory of Muret—and populace passed through

it during the vigour of the Middle Ages.
It dried up with the final corruption of mediæval
civilisation. The site became deserted and half
forgotten. But in our own time, just within
living memory, a Bishop of Cahors revived it,
and his efforts had a more far-reaching result than
he had hoped for. It was as though a lamp, in
which the oil was believed exhausted, being re-
lighted, should burn with a brilliant flame.
Nothing pictorial, certainly nothing descriptive
in writing, can give fully the individual effect of
the place. The platform in front of the three
superimposed chapels, the tall building of the
monastery above, plastered to the rock, the castle
well towards the summit, the narrow town hanging far below, the whole thing resembling a
ladder on a natural outline of broken rock against
the sky rather than the work of man.

Since the first effect of that vision is one of the
most remarkable in Europe, I advise everyone
who visits it to approach it in the particular
manner which has been made most feasible
through the advent of the railway. The approach
should be across the edge of the *causse* or plateau
from the east, whether you journey on foot or by
car, until you come to the little hamlet called
Hospitalet at the edge of the cliff. There halt a
moment, and instead of going forward to the edge
(as yet you see nothing) turn somewhat to the left
above the highroad which runs down to its

tunnel through the rock. There, before you get to the tunnel, or just above it, the valley opens before you and the precipice of Rocamadour rises against the green distant hills : a cascade of building, or a clambering of stones, one upon the shoulders of another, mingling with and fretting the sheer rock, as the details of a Gothic ruin against the sky fret the main perpendicular line of it : a sight that no one who has seen it will forget, and which no one will feel so keenly who has come upon Rocamadour from the west or north. Most of the great shrines in Europe have this natural appeal of landscape—as you may test at Chartres if, again, you come in the right way from the Beauce by the William Gate—and perhaps it is only in our own age that this appeal has been overlooked. Perhaps in some future day it will be recaptured.

PÉRIGUEUX is a town the quality of which lies in its possession of two kinds of monuments : one of a sort which you may find scattered up and down throughout western Europe, and particularly throughout France ; the other unique, peculiar to the place itself.

What Périgueux has in common with so many other towns is a Roman foundation, or necleus, and a considerable body of mediæval remains to which one must add one or two very fine bits of the Renaissance. What it has quite peculiar to itself and unlike any other monument I know in the West, is the Church of St. Front, which one does not know whether to call an invasion of the Orient into the heart of France, with no forerunners and no trace of the way by which it came, or a characteristic creation of the Western mind inspired by some vague memory or some fleeting suggestion which that mind had recorded from the architecture of the East.

Périgueux was Vesona, the capital of a countryside in the hills standing on the bend of a river in the middle of fruitful but wooded country—the

PERIGUEUX.

To face page 150.

great roads pass to the east or to the west of this central tumbled land and not through it. Why it should have been so considerable a centre, first, probably, in independent Gaul, later, certainly, in Roman Gaul, we cannot tell. But the town still bears all the marks of its Roman foundation. It is a true Roman provincial capital, and has rightly given its name to the whole district of the Périgord. The Roman amphitheatre, used as a quarry for so many generations, has still some of the lower courses of its oval wall remaining, though in ruin ; one or two arches stand, and the foundations of its ellipse are completely marked out. The trace of the Roman city is still everywhere apparent, and one may say, I think, that only one element of such origin is lacking ; one cannot clearly see what it was that made the citadel ; there is no defined stronghold site in the whole place. But the Roman air and the Roman tradition remain.

Of the Middle Ages you find examples at every turn, unexpected and striking enough. The late mediæval corner tower of the outer wall stands intact ; the houses, which still bear their pointed turrets here and there, the names of the narrower streets, with ogives of the thirteenth and four-teenth centuries, built into the mass of many older buildings ; while the Renaissance has one particularly fine example : some wealthy burgher's house standing upon the riverside by

the end of the chief bridge—as perfect in its
miniature way as the things of the Loire. For
Périgueux was that which the Revolution has
everywhere marred and crippled, a vivid centre
of local life ; nor would any social reform be of
greater advantage to the French to-day than the
reorganisation of local freedoms which should
give to these provincial capitals a new and
vigorous life such as they possessed for so many
centuries until the change of a hundred and thirty
years ago, clinched as it was by the mathematical
genius of Napoleon, centralised and newly
ordered all things.

You will find in Périgueux a statue erected to
the memory of Montaigne, upon the pedestal of
which is a citation from his pen, which citation
exactly expresses the pride of the old provincial
capitals in their local life :

> I would rather be the first man in Périgueux than
> the second or the third in Paris.

No man feels that to-day !

I have said that the peculiar and unique thing
about Périgueux was the Church of St. Front ;
and to discover how special a case it is, how much
a thing of its own kind, not to be paralleled anywhere else in the West, consider this : that
wherever else you go throughout Gaul, you find
the regular plan of the old Roman Church changing with the early Middle Ages into the pointed
Gothic and later into the quite new type of the

PERIGUEUX : A TYPICAL FEATURE ON THE ASCENT TO THE CATHEDRAL.

To face page 152.

Renaissance. But here the domes are not of Gaul at all, but of the Orient ; the domes and the campanile are such as you might never find farther west than Padua or Venice. You say as you first see them that they came thither from the eastern Mediterranean, and that Byzantium was their origin ; and you are right. But in the great Church of St. Front you have this second consideration, that the character of the Orient has disappeared. In detail, in spirit, even in main effect, it is not at all from beyond the Adriatic ; it is rather as though some one had seen the things of the eastern Mediterranean once vividly in youth, and had come back with a mere memory of them in his mind, and setting out under that influence to build, had built that which he could not help making a Western thing. Nowhere is there the least trace of a re-entrant curve : nowhere is there that characteristic of all things Oriental, an attempt at lightness. The huge church, in its modern restoration as much as in its original decayed stones, has about it the characteristics of our Western race and culture—strength, density, and the ponderous stuff which is determined upon eternity. It does not lift, it imposes. The five great domes are of massive stones. The high, square bell tower dominating them is of huge square blocks. The ornamentation is insignificant and conventional. The keynote everywhere is the round arch and nothing

153

but the round arch, from which endless combinations are formed merely by imposing variations upon this seemingly monotonous and essentially austere theme.

There is within the church a modern mosaic, not very distinguishable, in front of one of the altars, the picture of an elephant, and under the mosaic in stone letters, ' *Fortitudo.*' That is St. Front : a magnificent animal of great purpose, planted for ever upon this slope above the river. As you look up to it from the waterside, it gives something of the effect of a cluster of rocks in its immensity and strength ; and, at any rate, there is nothing of its kind elsewhere. It stirs me strangely to sit in that nave and consider the weight that here reposes upon the rock. Here is no facing of marble upon brick, no encrustation, no filling in of parallel walls with rubble, no thin curtain, no drawn-out pilasters. Here is one simple pile of titanic masonry square shafts yards thick, plain semicircular ridges, the width of a palace vault across. All the large semicircular arches are of thick stone, and all the mighty domes as well. Everywhere one scheme of line, the perpendicular, the horizontal, and the semicircular, worked into imposingly symmetrical designs, and everywhere one material and one only.

There has been plenty of blame offered to those who thus decided to renew the old church and to make it weatherproof again after its hundreds of years—so that now you can hardly tell where an old Stone is to be found, at any rate, in its outer Structure—but, for my part, I am glad that they have acted so. Give it another thousand years, and St. Front will be a witness to a thousand years ago, for it was built before the Crusades. Give it another thousand years after this modern reStoration—perhaps our civilisation will not be capable of much more work upon this scale, for we are already in peril of decline—give it another thousand years, and men, forgetting that it was ever reStored, will say to themselves, ' Here is a thing of twenty centuries, Stark with the spirit of the Dark Ages, unornamented, enormous, proclaiming certitude, and therefore a juSt emblem of the spirits which designed it.'

I say men will speak thus. But I am not so sure that all these generations hence there will be enough left of our culture to allow them to use any such language. There is so much of mediæval lore and culture of which we of to-day have been able to underStand but a little, that it is only reasonable to expeét the next thousand years to obscure the vistas of the paSt as callously as have the two centuries juSt ended. It is more likely that those men of the future will speak of such things as the ' work of the ancients ' and will worship them without any recolleétions of their origins.

CHAPTER XXI

THE GREAT HOUSE OF DURTAL

I KNOW not why it is, but there are many places which, through the mechanical accidents of our time, become overknown, and others which one might call underknown. Too many people know Assisi; not nearly enough people know Loretto. Too many people know Rabat and Fez, even to-day. Too many people know Montserrat, and not enough know the Chimneys of Riglos, which are among the wonders of the world.

Durtal, the Great House of Durtal, is one of the lesser known things. Perhaps I ought to be glad of that, for I can easily imagine it ruined by crowds. But, at any rate, if it has pride in itself, or if its ghostly owners could feel human pride in whatever place they now may be, it seems unfair that such a thing should not be as famous to-day as it most assuredly is splendid.

The Great House of Durtal is a lesser example of the spirit which, when it had all the wealth of the kingship behind it, set up those neighbouring castles of the Loire which are certainly among the much too well-known things. Durtal

DURTAL
Forrest Whome
June 1896

THE HOUSE OF DURTAL.

To face page 156.

had no such wealth behind it ; it was the great house of a big private gentleman. But Lord, what an effect he got for his money ! You will look in vain, I think, for any other private house in Europe, in the countrysides, at least—for I do not know whether one should call the Barberini House a palace or not—which gives you such an impression of nobility, of magnificence ; in the old sense of the term magnificence : ' A great doing—a making of something worthy.'

The builder played every trick—and legitimately—to give this effect of magnificence. When first the place had been set up as a stronghold, in the Dark Ages when all such strongholds were founded, a knoll above the quiet river had been castellated. It was the castle of Durtal ; but when greater wealth and less power came to the descendants of that house, the falling ground was fronted with a projecting three sides of Renaissance work which makes to-day the Great House of Durtal, three piled up stories high above the low-lying ground to the south ; but on the north, at the top of the steep hill the ground on a level with its second storey. The builder spread out the stone basement of that cliff of a façade at an angle, after the fashion of the Egyptians, to give a look of support and strength to the weight above ; and in the eastern corner he married the high Renaissance roof to the last battlements of the Middle Ages, just as the builders of the

Medicean Louvre in Paris joined the Middle Ages to sixteenth-century Italy.

One would have thought that Durtal would have been famous if through Rabelais alone, for all the glorious episode of Picrochole turns upon Durtal; he was Lord of Durtal, if you remember, when he was struck with that sudden burst of imperialism of his and determined to conquer the whole world ' without fear of being turned upon his flank by the Muscovites.'

But Rabelais has brought no fame to this, and for a hundred who see the master in bronze upon the public place of Chinon, scarcely one, I suppose, has ever seen Durtal.

Perhaps the choice of travellers is wise, for Durtal is dead, in spite of all its beauty and strength. These things were intended for human habitations and for lordships. They went with personal powers and personal prides. They have now no functions to fulfil, because the builders of them have departed and their descendants inhabit them no more. You may go through the halls of that old place and find no ornament; the promise of the great façade is not fulfilled within; one wing at the back which closed the courtyard has disappeared; and as for using the place, it has been turned into a hospital. Durtal is no longer Durtal, because it is no longer alive. But it is worth seeing, all the same, and if a man wants a series in which the history of

DURTAL

THE HOUSE OF DURTAL: A COURTYARD ABOVE THE VAULTED
CELLARS.

To face page 158.

all our vivid developments between the Crusades and the Reformation may stand before him, let him visit Durtal after Angers—an hour in the local train and less in a motor. He will see at Angers—and he will be wise to approach from the river—a castle of stark bastions, wholly devoid of any grace at all, a great quadrilateral of half-round towers, not very high, gigantically thick and strong, with hardly a slit for light or for arrows round the wall, built, too early for battlements, of a dark and forbidding stone which you can hardly distinguish from the rock out of which it springs and into which it is dovetailed. Angers, though it is the Plantagenet castle in which first were heard the songs of the Arthurian cycle, within the gaunt naked walls of which arose the beginnings of the Middle Ages, is built wholly for use, and for one use—the use of war ; and of war when war meant the rumbling of mangonel engines attempting to batter down walls almost as strong as the walls of nature. Angers is sheerly for defence, the stronghold of a man who was a king. Then came the great four hundred years of development, and at the end of them, Durtal, no longer a castle in the old sense at all, not built for defence nor suggesting it, yet still suggesting strength and, above all, power of tradition.

I sometimes wonder, when I see the way in which the rich build nowadays, failing nearly always to reach the effect they desire, that they do not merely copy. Why has not some one of our modern rich set to work to reproduce Durtal? He would certainly have a house better than anything they have built in Europe for two hundred years. But I suppose when he had done it some other revolution like that which has taken the soul out of Durtal would nullify his efforts, and that the palace which he had raised for the satisfaction of his vanity or of his legitimate pride in blood would be debased to false uses in its turn.

At any rate, there is Durtal, as good a thing in death as I know. Perhaps some rich man with a kind heart will buy it back from the governors of the hospital, destroy in it the devices of the religious who tend the sick, turn its chapel into a dancing hall, re-erect the fallen north wing, complete the courtyard again, and fill Durtal once more with a false life. And if that happens I know not whether I shall be glad or sorry.

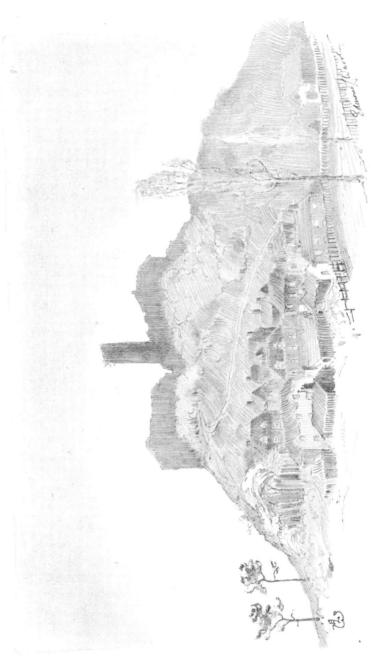

CHALUS.

CHAPTER XXII

CHALUS

THERE are places in Europe of great interest to English history, of which most of us have read in the text-books, and which not many Englishmen know. Either they are too small or too remote or they lie off the great line of steam travel—from which modern petrol has not yet learned to go—or they are taken for granted as names and no more ; but for whatever reason, such they are, and numerous. The battle-field of Crécy is but a mile or two off the track of everyone who motors down into France from Boulogne, every yard of which is known. It is to-day what it was when the battle was fought nearly six hundred years ago. But it is almost unknown ; and the same is true of Taillebourg and the same of Agincourt.

Now there is one spot which I had always desired to visit, and yet I had only managed to gratify that desire this year : that spot is Chalus, where Richard the Lion-Heart was killed. It was a death which was in keeping with his life. The king of death which a contemporary might have been certain he would have died, for with all his ill health and continuous travel, he could hardly have died save under arms. It was in the Limousin just where the hills of that province sink into the western plain. There had been treasure-trove. The Viscount of Limoges claimed it; King Richard as his overlord counter-claimed. The vassal shut up the treasure in his castle of Chalus, there to defend it and defy his lord. Richard came against it with his small, trained mercenary force and laid siege. A plain arrow with a square iron tip—what was called in the French of his day a *quarrel*—struck him down from the walls as he was riding around inspecting those defences. He did not die immediately. He died because the wound was ill dressed and only after a few days. He lived to see the place fall, and the man who had shot him down captured. But although pardoned, after the king's death the bowman was flayed alive by the family.

The place where the greatest man of his time in Europe fell is to-day a small, half-neglected little country town—for it has a market—yet half village; and what is left of that stronghold, in the capture of which Richard met his death, is still exceedingly impressive. One sees upon visiting it why Limoges had made it the test of his power and gave his challenge there to the man who controlled all the resources of England and half those of France. Not that it was very large.

Chalus
June 4
1926

CHALUS : THE OUTER WARD.

To face page 163.

It was the better for being restricted in space and
needing no great garrison to feed. Nor was it
so very difficult of general approach, but it was
exactly suited for a fortress of that day, chosen
as were all Richard's fortified sites (Château
Gaillard is the best known) with the skill of the
master. Unlike Château Gaillard, however, there
is no height nearby from which it can be dominated by the eye, nor is the mount of Chalus
connected, as is Château Gaillard, by a neck or
isthmus with higher land—as of necessity were
the greater part of these keeps. It stood upon a
low, conical hill, steep enough to break the
attack, yet spread out enough to allow sallies to
some distance from the walls. At its foot runs
a stream which was something of an obstacle,
and beyond that stream, as a sort of bastion, those
who planned the castle had built an outer ward
covering the only bridge. The bridge still
stands, or rather, after much patching and changing, the bridge of to-day is still on the site of the
old one. Of the outer walls, the main tower
still dominates the village ; and within the remains of its walls, some few houses are huddled.
The gateway into the outer yard under this main
tower is intact. The outline of the main stronghold upon the hill over the river can everywhere
be traced, though it has lost its height. A farm-
house of perhaps the fifteenth or sixteenth century
has been built, backed against its walls. The old

keep tower on the summit reaches to its full
height, but is half ruined ; at the side next it a
gateway and perhaps a chapel, of a much later
date toward the end of the Middle Ages, retain
an arch or two and half a roof. The rest is without habitation and is a ruin.

Nevertheless, the aspect of the place is still in
the highest degree impressive, and its purpose as
a fortress is insistent to the eye when one stands
in the meadows to the west, looking toward the
distant foothills of the Limousin. Those two
towers, the lower one of the outer ward, and the
higher hill of the main keep on the far side of the
stream, stand up at the main outlines of the place.
Even the spire of the church is subservient to
them, and the lines of the roofs of the little
market towns have all the effect of something
created by the original strength of a stronghold,
something which existed under the protection of
that lordship and which had been created by it.

Whether as tradition, or because some one had
wandered there and spoken of the story of the
place, I found the memory of the king alive. In
that remote inn which pretends to nothing, and
is therefore comfortable and good, they knew so
much. But there was no full tradition with
which to compare, for instance, the tradition of
Falaise, where the Conqueror colours the whole
town, or with the tradition of Mauperthuis Farm
and the Battle of Poitiers. All they knew was

that Richard the Lion-Heart, whose name I suppose will always live in western Europe, had been killed under their walls : but they thought of him as a foreigner. Yet when he fell there under those walls, he fell as Duke of Aquitaine, he was Angevin, a Plantagenet who spoke the language of their lords and could even understand perhaps the southern dialect of the populace round about. Happily enough, I found the memory of this most attractive son in the great brood of Mélisande more remembered in Agen, far off on the Garonne, than here in the place where he should be most famous. For at Agen I found a street named after him, and at the end of the bridge over the Garonne a tablet proudly inscribed with the legend that Richard, King of England, Duke of Aquitaine, had been the first to span the river, and that they owed their first bridge to him. Many wars have since destroyed it, and in its place—of all things in the world—there is now a rickety suspension bridge, built in the days when these hideous contrivances were thought marvellous.

If I were mayor of Chalus, I would erect a monument to Richard. It is not a small thing, the site where a great man dies ; and yet, if you will consider it, all up and down Europe, the places where men have achieved this or that action are rather noted, but rarely the place where they came by some great death : that which was chief in their own experience, and the closing of that experience, posterity forgets. At Chinon they remember Joan of Arc and Rabelais, but not Henry of Anjou, who died within the walls above the town mourning that he was a conquered king. There is nothing to mark, in the suburbs of Nancy, the place where Charles the Bold was dragged from his horse. There is a stone in the New Forest for the detestable Rufus, but nothing, I believe, in the rough fields which mark the site of the Hall of Fotheringay. And so it is with the place where Richard of England died. Yet I think he himself would rather have a memorial here even than at Acre, or at Jaffa, or in that village where he lay ill, despairing of seeing Jerusalem which lay not a day's march away.

Irony fills all history—and it has given the Lion-Heart a statue in front of the Victorian House of Lords in London and made him look like an English gentleman of the Albert period : but in Chalus there is not a bronze or a stone.

VIRE.
Edmund Havre

VIRE.

To face page 167.

CHAPTER XXIII

VIRE

I THINK the Norman towns, especially the
smaller ones, lose half their interest for the
traveller if he does not know the peculiar
history of the duchy and the way in which it stood
out as a separate thing in European history for
nearly five hundred years, and is something still
distinct among the French provinces. Even as
it is, the lesser towns of Normandy are singularly
little known, considering how easy of access they
are, how hospitable, and how charming. And
Vire, although it lies on one of the main railway
lines, is little visited.

Like nearly all Norman towns, you must understand it as a feudal fortress. Roughly speaking,
there are two types of towns in western Europe—
I mean towns with any tradition and antiquity.
They are either natural mercantile centres—for
instance, the first bridge across a great river with
sea-borne commerce, such as is Rouen or even
Caen (though there the river is small)—or they
are towns the sites of which were chosen because,
under the conditions of the time in which they
arose, they had good opportunity for defence.

167

The towns which were mercantile centres and early became large places were fortified in spite of their position; the sea-ports, for instance, Dieppe and Harfleur—now high and dry—and Honfleur opposite; and towns like Bayeux were fortified in spite of the difficulties of defence in order to protect their wealth; but nearly all the other Norman ones were first chosen for their defensive position.

So you must begin at Vire, as you should begin in so many other places, by taking what is left of the castle for your starting point in the understanding of the town. Massive ruined walls still remain as the relics of the keep which Henry of England, the son of the Conqueror, first put up in this place. It stands on its granite rock, plumb over the ravine of the River Vire below, and was the making of the place. Next you will note here and there, remaining in isolated sections and half ruined, individual towers built into later buildings, the ramparts, and the gates. One famous gate still stands, called the Gate of the Tower. It was on a height from which any approach to the little city could be spotted by watchers for miles around. From the summit of it you saw to the south the wide range above Sourdeval (Sourdeval was the lordship of the first man to leap upon the wall of Jerusalem in the first Crusade); and to the north, all the country of the Bocage—that district of lower Normandy

Vire
The Clock Tower
and fortified Gateway

Edmund Warre

VIRE : THE TOWER GATE.

To face page 168.

which, being hilly and densely wooded, kept its ancient customs longest. It was the last place to witness a revolt against national taxation by the king—as late as Louis XIV.

Of this tower gate the people of Vire are proud enough ; they have decorated it on numberless occasions ; as late as the seventeenth century they put up a statue of Our Lady above the arch, and it is to be prayed that they will never pierce streets round it, as men have done with so many other of the old narrow gateways of Europe—as for instance, at Southampton. For its whole character and all its architectural effect lie in the way it blocks the narrow street and forms a true defensible entry.

Vire has ventured, and not unsuccessfully, little manufactories, but happily without hurting its soul in any way ; and it has managed not to deteriorate, in spite of any number of temptations ; not even the motor car has done it evil, and you can hardly say that of any other such town, except perhaps its sister, Mortain, over the hills to the south beyond Sourdeval.

Even if it had no history, all that district would still be a delight ; and anyone with leisure who wants to understand lower Normandy may take Vire for his centre and learn more and more of what age and tradition mean in things European. He is within a walk of Mortain and its cascade and its old headship of a county, now half forgotten; within a walk of Avranches, and the superb view over St. Michael's Bay; within a walk of the battlefield of Tinchebrai; and in Vire itself he has a whole collection of mediæval and Renaissance heirlooms to please him—the granite church with its vivid sculpture, the ruin of the second gate, the famous little valley below, the half-dozen Renaissance or very late mediæval private buildings testifying to the wealth of the place.

And it is still wealthy. It is one of the chief pleasures of these small old Norman towns that they have not lost, as have towns in many European countries, their quality of local residence. They are not the tiny capitals they once were; it is no longer a necessity for the gentry round about to make such places their centres of provision and their meeting-place for neighbours; but the wealth, made in the town itself and the surroundings, is still spent for the most part in Vire. And it is this which gives life to the older places of Europe; lacking it, when they fall under the industrial system of the new economic era, they must inevitably forfeit their personality.

The way in which Vire keeps its soul and independence, in which Vire lives on, feeling prouder than its little sister towns, is due to the effect of eight hundred years of custom now forgotten—but during all these centuries an essential of the place : it was royal ; it had no local lord. Vire was the ' Duke's Town,' small as it was ; and when Normandy fell to the crown, it was the ' King's Town.' Vire does not know to-day why it is still proud. That is the reason. But even if it did know, it would scarcely pay any heed, for its pride has become a thing of interminable habit, self-sustaining, and self-augmenting as time goes on. It has always been moved by an independence surpassed at last only by patriotism. It has obeyed no master save the ruler of its peers. And those who are alive to history feel that spirit in its streets to-day.

L E MANS is a name newly familiar. It was, if I am not mistaken, an American base during the war. I know, at any rate, that the presence of the American Army there is well remembered. Save for that episode, however, it is not one of the better-known towns of northern France to-day, though it, again, lies on one of the great lines of travel, and on one of the chief railways connecting Paris with the Atlantic—the railway to Brest. It is that which gave it the economic and (after a fashion) strategic position which it held during the Great War. But, normally, the communications of western Europe through the Atlantic leave Le Mans by the way. Goods and men come off the ships at Cherbourg or at Havre, and the lines thence to Paris leave Le Mans far to the west. Meanwhile, the normal roads of travel from the north to the south of Europe also neglect it. They converge on Paris from the ports of Normandy and of Picardy ; they radiate out from Paris to Bordeaux and to Marseilles. Le Mans has enjoyed one advantage from this position :

172

Le Mans

LE MANS

To face page 172.

it has retained its spirit; and though it has largely forgotten its own history, one can—as one grasps the character of the old town, masked by the extension of modern building—recall the original plan and the castle rock which was the heart of Maine.

Normandy, with its intense history, was the Roman Province of the Second Lyonnaise. Brittany was the Celtic Province which, though it was and is half Roman-speaking, preserved and preserves a life entirely its own. Normandy ever attempted to master Brittany. The dukes of Normandy were for ever desiring to obtain an acknowledgment of their supremacy from the rulers of Brittany. The two provinces, which then were virtually kingdoms, touched in the Bay of Saint-Michel; but the wilder western land never submitted. It only played at submission to Rouen in order to avoid submission to Paris.

Wedged in between the two, just below the sea-coast and not having access to the sea; lozenge-shaped, not wholly of Anjou, not stretching to the Loire; formed, we know not how, by the petty local lordships of the darkness after Charlemagne, there rose up that countryside of Maine whose function it was to be a march land between the Breton and the Norman power. In all their history, until the final consolidation of the French monarchy at the end of the Middle

Ages, Maine was the makeweight and the balance. William the Conqueror insisted upon ruling it, and took, by dint of great effort, its capital, Le Mans. Four hundred years later, as the Plantagenet line was failing, the cession of Maine was felt in England to be the peril of Normandy, and the man who had sacrificed Maine as the price of Henry VI.'s marriage paid for the sacrifice with his life. And even to-day, when all these things are forgotten, Maine and Le Mans play a neutral rôle. They are not Norman, and they are not Breton ; and modern travel which knows Normandy and Brittany by heart misses Maine and its capital—to their good.

I have just called Le Mans a hill town. I suppose that most of my contemporaries who visit it will think I am using some special term of my own not corresponding to reality. The land rises slowly from the Huisne ; that there was ever here a citadel, a defensible place, one might not guess, especially if one should come in from the railway station on the flat, or by the road from Angers, or from the south. But to understand what Le Mans means in history, do not, upon arriving there, go straight into the centre of the city, but rather cross the Sarthe westward, and thence, from the suburb on the right bank of the river, look up against the steep hill—it is almost a cliff—on which the castle (what is left of it) and the cathedral stand. Thence you will see what

174

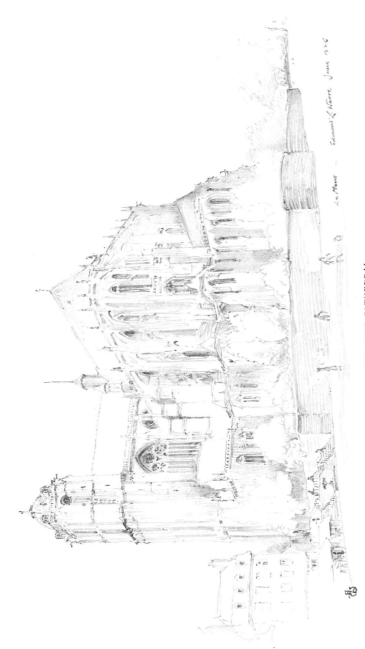

LE MANS : THE CATHEDRAL.

To face page 175.

Le Mans meant to our fathers. It was by river that trade came to the place ; it was by river that stores of war could be accumulated within it. Seen thus, standing above the river, it is a splendid steep. Even on the far side toward the east there was, in the first state of the countryside, before any levelling or building up, an approach upon a slope, defensible by a wall, and old Le Mans stood within a circle of walls which had that steep rock fall upon the water for its highest point, and looked down from that at the precipitous slopes. See how to-day the modern street cuts through the rock citadel by a tunnel ; and see how the castle, now reduced to a governor's residence of the later Middle Ages, its old strength quite forgotten, still masters the stream, and how the cathedral towers above the whole.

That building, the cathedral of Le Mans, is thought the most perfect of the later Gothic churches in France. From within, looking toward the choir, it is certainly that ; and from without, looking at the great sheaf of flying buttresses, it is that no less. But there is another feature in the great pile which a wise man will note for himself if he will go and stand in the little square of the bishopric above the steps which lead to the old dominating rock that brought Le Mans into being ; thence he will see in one view the half-barbaric western front, grotesque with the heavy and terrifying humour of the

175

eleventh century or the early twelfth, before the architecture of the West had caught the flame ; and in that same view he sees something older than any Christian church, the great druidical stone, built right into the walls ; and in that same view he sees the superb south transept, the last achievement of the Gothic.

There is another thing in Le Mans, not commonly known, which always moves me profoundly ; that is the tomb of Berengaria, the woman whom Richard the Lion-Heart loved, and for whom he broke with the house of France, repudiating the sister of the King. Why she comes to lie there, while he is at Fontevrault, I do not know ; but there she lies, three weeks' march northward from her father's land, the queen and the mate of the greatest man of her time who had died so long before her by that blunt arrow under Chalus, days and days away. If I knew nothing in Le Mans except her tomb, I should think the place worth visiting for that alone.

Part V
The Rhine March

AIX-LA-CHAPELLE : THE FISH MARKET AND CATHEDRAL.

To face page 179.

CHAPTER XXV

AIX-LA-CHAPELLE

THE Rhine March, the broad belt of country lying to the left or west of the middle and lower navigable Rhine, has been for centuries the very heart of European political debate.

It is an accident of our generation that the debate should ever seem settled. The sudden and complete victory won by Prussia and her allies over France in 1870, and the consequent amalgamation of more than two-thirds of the Germans under the leadership of Prussia, the creation thereby of a state which has come to be called ' Germany ' (though it does not include anything like the totality of the German culture) —these things between them seemed to have settled the debate for good.

The gradually weakening demands of the French for the restoration of Metz and Strasbourg, with their provinces, were the only exception to this apparently fixed settlement. It was always thought to be a particular French grievance, little understood or sympathised with elsewhere, and, as I have said, it was rapidly dying down.

But the Great War brought back vividly before

179

Europe, as a whole, the critical character of this belt of country. A modern man would speak of that critical character as a quarrel between France and Germany—France desiring a hold upon the Rhine to secure itself from invasion, and Germany desiring complete control over it for the simple reason that, with the exception of a very small district round Metz, the whole is German-speaking; while even this district round Metz had been welded by the impression and increasing wealth of nearly fifty years into the new Prussianised Reich.

But this common, modern way of talking of the present debate is very superficial and very provincial, confined to conditions of no long standing, and not likely to have long endurance. It is something very much deeper than the rivalry between a modern German state and a modern French state, which is at work in all this countryside. Briefly, the fate of the Rhineland has turned upon these two divergent conditions : it is German; but it is of Roman foundation. An Englishman might note with interest an almost exactly parallel case on the border and in the southern lowlands of Scotland. They also were Romanised, and had their foundation in the Roman Empire; but they were attached to a nation all the farther part of which had never been administered by the civilisation of antiquity. Hence the perpetual attempts of the English

AIX-LA-CHAPELLE : THE SHRINE.

To face page 180.

Government to hold, or at least influence, this nearer part of Scotland, and hence its 'Anglification' during and after the eleventh century.

It is in the same way that the Rhine March, though essentially German in language, culture, and, upon the whole, in race, has another spiritual strain in it and another historical memory, and goes back to a very different foundation from the Germany which stands round the Elbe.

All the innumerable results of this double-origin would take volumes to discuss. I propose to do no more than what a chance traveller may do in the description of certain of its typical cities, and especially of their chief buildings; for in them one has presented to the eye the whole past of the country, and its inward nature coming out in stone. I have chosen six such towns—Aix, Metz and Treves, Bonn, Worms and Spires. I begin with Aix and Metz because these two, lying right on the border of the Rhine March, the one German-speaking from the beginning, the other Latin and French-speaking for two thousand years, are typical of the March, the border, towns.

I may add that I propose to follow the old custom of giving foreign towns their English names, and not the modern (and, I hope, passing) habit of spelling them as they are spelt by their inhabitants. I would as soon talk of *Aachen* as I would talk of *Paree* or *Lyong*.

Aix is the town of Charlemagne. His presence

overshadows the place ; he is buried in the heart of it ; he is the influence, or the ghost, or the god of the city. He was brought up, indeed, at his family's place in Aix and at another which they had at Metz, so that presumably the servants about his childhood were German-speaking in the one case, and spoke a low Latin dialect in the other. I verily believe that it is this influence of the man in whom was summed up all that was left of antiquity and all the beginnings of the Middle Ages, which gives Aix its singular dignity. Nowhere else have I seen modern work so admirably fitted in with the old except in certain architectural experiments of the two English universities.

The shrine itself, the cathedral under which the great emperor lies, is an exact and harmonious mixture of the oldest and the latest things. There is not a jarring note ; and all the accessories of that triumph in stone and mosaic are the same. Nowhere have I heard music more solemnly fulfilling its part in a Christian church, and no-where has modern restoration seemed, in my eyes, at least, more successful. The candle ring of gilt bronze, a sort of crown dependent from the roof, goes back to Barbarossa. The mosaics of the dome are of the other day—not forty years old, from the hands, I believe, of Italian workmen. Of the pillars supporting the roof and arches of the gallery most are original, some few brought

AIX-LA-CHAPELLE : THE MARCH GATE.

To face page 182.

AIX-LA-CHAPELLE : THE MARCH GATE.

To face page 183.

in in our time to complete the work. Yet they produce an effect of complete unity. And in the midst of that gallery, facing the high altar and the choir, on its arcade above the people, stands the throne of Charlemagne ; the plain, white marble chair, which brings the mind back at once to the Chair of St. Peter in Rome. Authority seated.

In the externals of the place I find the same unity between what was old and what is new. The eye can follow in the last courses of the original octagonal church material which is Roman. It discovers in the round windows of those walls the ancient unchanging spirit which ran through the Dark Ages until the Gothic Renaissance. It is surprising that a thirteenth- and fourteenth-century choir in the pure French-Gothic attached to this Romanesque and much more modern thing in no way swears with it, and seems a natural completion, and (what is, perhaps, more remarkable) the odd seventeenth-century roof, with its eight separate ridges like the sections of an open orange, makes no jarring effect. And all the modern reconstruction of the open bridge from the western towers to the dome, and the modern replacement of sculpture and other detail, leaves the thing not only unspoiled, but the better. It is as though the unchanging character of European unity underlying all our shifting divisions, and summed up in the name of Charlemagne, had come forth and expressed itself visibly upon the shrine where he is buried.

This singular dignity, and what I have called ' success ' in the spirit of Aix, you find not only in the way it has treated its great central shrine, but in the restoration of its few remaining ancient buildings, and in the completely modern mass of its Town Hall. The old March Gate has been restored from a half-ruined state, completely in our own time, yet fails in nothing. It simply reproduces what the building was when it left the hands of its first builders.

The Town Hall is still more modern. When one considers what our time has done with its attempts to revive or copy a spirit which it thinks long dead, when one remembers the false Gothic of Châteauroux, for instance, and a hundred things in England, which are too familiar to us all, I marvel that this work at Aix should have been done as well as it has been.

In this same town of Aix there is a railway station which will show you what an attempt to be original and to break with tradition can achieve in the way of abomination. That was because the railway station was built for, by, and under the spirit of monstrous new doctrines from the Prussian East—if doctrine it can be called, for it is rather chaos. But here in the Town Hall, where Aix has its own spirit at work, you have the real German soul in architecture, the delight

184

AIX-LA-CHAPELLE : RATHAUS.

To face page 184.

in great roofs and somewhat fantastic towers, in romantic outlines, and in a pleasing extravagance making mystery of the whole. To use the same word again, this architecture ' succeeds.' Of the various towns of the Rhine March it is to Aix that I would always return for the sense of unfathomed antiquity, continuity, government. Round the old city there has grown up a vast new population, unhappily industrial, and created by the new mechanical expansion of the last fifty years. That has happened to many another old city, the whole point and meaning of which lay in its antiquity. It has happened to Oxford. It has happened to Rouen. But here in Aix it seemed to me, as I travelled through, not to have destroyed the meaning of the old, and not to be at enmity with it or to threaten it for the future. I may be wrong ; the spirit of modern competitive commerce is capable of anything in its lack of intelligence. So far it has spared Aix ; and may Aix be spared for ever.

CHAPTER XXVI

METZ

METZ is the pendant of Aix-la-Chapelle. They are the two typical frontier towns of the Rhine March : Aix German-speaking, Metz originally French-speaking, neither of them more than on the fringe of the German culture, yet neither of them divorced from that long series of accidents whereby the civilisation of the Roman Empire and its Faith penetrated beyond the great river, created mediæval Germany, and left, oddly attached in theory to the mediæval imperial crown, broad belts of land—extending as far as Lyons—which had never had any neighbourhood or connection with the German tongue.

Metz was one of the ' Three Bishoprics,' all of them French-speaking, all of them fortified towns from the very beginnings of history, until the Great War ; all of them showing the changes of fortification, phase after phase of that art, from the Roman wall of the later Empire to the ring of detached forts—' the entrenched camp,' as the French called it—which was the system of modern defence until the airplane (directing new

186

METZ CATHEDRAL.

To face page 186.

artillery) destroyed it and has replaced it for the moment by field works.

These three bishoprics are Verdun, Metz and Toul. The third (like Montreuil) escaped regular siege and fame in war for centuries, and the vast sums spent upon its use as a stronghold were thrown away, as they have been thrown away upon those successive modern navies which grow obsolete without engagement. But Verdun and Metz are of the first place in military history. The first most recent in our ears; the second equally famous to the generation before our own, through the battles and siege of 1870.

I have visited Metz over and over again during the last thirty-five years, ever since my boyhood : under the German occupation a score of times, and, since the Armistice, perhaps half-a-dozen.

What has struck me most there has been the effect of modern, compulsory education, a system universally applied in Western countries to the mass of the people, and only escaped by the well-to-do. Here in Metz it is possible to get an object lesson of what that crushing, uniform social machine can accomplish. Every building in Metz, save a few—artificial, deliberately intruded, to which I will allude in a moment—is as French as Nancy, Paris or Nantes. The cathedral is a typical piece of French Gothic, without a trace of other influence. You might find it in Amiens or Beauvais. The private houses have exactly the same mark. The cooking (that excellent test of popular culture) is, and has always been, French. The methods of agriculture around the city are French. The script in familiar writing is French—everything of men's lives is French to the marrow. Yet in the streets of Metz to-day you continually hear German. The popular newspaper is printed in German, and I think it is true to say that the mass of the people now *think* in German. If you were merely to count numbers and not influence, you might call Metz a half-German town in its speech. I may be wrong here, and those who know the town thoroughly can correct me if I am ; but certainly the impression of a frequent visitor is at least of a half-Germanisation of local language.

Now this has been brought about by the steam-roller effect of the compulsory elementary school. I can remember Metz a French-speaking town.

To-day you have the unnatural picture of a town, perhaps mainly, or at any rate half, German-speaking, though it remains in everything but speech as French as ever. It has all come about in one generation. Of course, the work will be undone by the reversing of the engine, and French will again take the place of German. It is the work of exactly one generation to effect either change. But what a lesson in the socialistic powers of the modern state and the impotence of the private citizen under a modern executive !

188

METZ: THE RIVERSIDE AND CATHEDRAL.

To face page 188.

Metz is as French as Canterbury is English. If you came back to Canterbury after an interval of thirty years and found it mainly French-speaking, yet still drinking English beer and eating English eggs and bacon and playing English cricket—let alone showing in nearly all its buildings the un-mistakable English type—you would have some parallel to what has happened at Metz; and the moral is not that a language easily changes, but that the modern state can do pretty well anything by compulsory education. We should do well to meditate upon that novel, arbitrary and tyrannical power.

I have said that the cathedral of Metz is essentially French. It is also one of the finest in the world. It was not ruined during the German occupation—whether because the original official architect was kept on or not I cannot tell—but, at any rate, though some few of its details were badly coarsened by unintelligent restoration, the building as a whole remains a magnificent and typical monument of the French Middle Ages. The glass has been admirably preserved, and under the German administration the interior, in its lesser decorations, was (in my judgment) improved. What mars the whole effect is a new western front.

The old western front was incongruous—but it was historical—it was a heavy, false Renaissance, French classical front, plastered on to the

Gothic of the rest; much as the front of St. Eustache in Paris was plastered on to the fine earlier marriage of Renaissance and Gothic in that Parish church. The addition was made to commemorate the voyage—which was half a pilgrimage—made by Louis XV to Metz in offering thanks for his recovery from illness. The Germans thought the incongruity must be removed, in spite of its historical meaning—or perhaps on account of that historical meaning. At any rate, they replaced it by a Gothic west front in the ordinary Gothic style, of which nothing need be said save that it appears much worse in combination with the ancient Gothic than did its utterly different predecessor : for the one was good in its own style and the other is not.

But what is enormous, unforgivable, grotesque and all the same exceedingly instructive in this new west front, and what ought to make it famous throughout the world, is a certain detail the like of which you will not see matched in Christendom. Of four figures of the Old Testament prophets (figures of heroic size which decorate this front), one, that of the Prophet Daniel, is the deliberately executed portrait of the Emperor William II ! There he is, with his ultra-modern face, his curled-up moustache, all the signs of what would be normal enough in a suit of dittos or the uniform of a Prussian general officer, but is absolutely stupefying in the robes and hood of

190

METZ : THE GERMAN GATE.

To face page 191.

a major prophet, and in the convention of the Middle Ages.

The German occupation made other less eccentric, but equally artificial, things. It planted a garrison church in the island suburb on the river, designed after a modern idea of the Rhenish roofs and towers. It put up one or two big shops in the dreadful fashion of Berlin ; a well-organised and hideous railway Station ; and, opposite it, a huge poSt office in that same fashion of a monstrous Aztec sort of carving which has been affeĉted throughout the German Empire, and which I have seen polluting architeĉture in the heart of Switzerland, and even as far south as Pola and Trieste.

One feature Metz has, and one only, which not only recalls the domeStic and military architeĉts of the Middle Ages, but has been, upon the whole, not so badly reStored by the alien Government which held it for so many years. It is the old gate of the ramparts to the eaSt, known as the *Porte d'Allemagne*, spanning an affluent of the Moselle and the deep ditch which formerly defended the city. It is a fine piece of work sufficiently preserved ; the modern reinforcement, made with fresh Stone, has not really spoilt it, and (what is important) no new Stone has been added where the old Stone would serve.

But Metz has a meaning and a lesson for the Statesman other than that to be drawn from its language, or from its external being. For it was the policy adopted with regard to Metz after the war of 1870 which led to the final disaster of Prussia and to that new arrangement of the German peoples which is not yet concluded, and the formation of which we are now witnessing.

For after the sudden and complete victories of the German armies under Prussian leadership fifty-seven years ago, the military party clamoured that, in the terms of peace, the annexation of Metz should be included. It is as certain as anything in modern history can be (and perhaps that is not saying much, seeing how secretly all things have been accomplished in our time) that the genius of Bismarck foresaw the perils that would result from this error. He threw all his weight into the scale against such a policy, but without avail. That great man, whom we may call the Prussian Richelieu, had grasped all the factors of the problem before him for the creation of a new Reich under the mastership of Prussia. He had luck, of course, as well; for without luck a great man cannot make his mark in international politics. But he had even more talent than good fortune. He grasped, before his time, the unifying effect upon the modern mind of a common language. He knew the gradual use to which so superficial a test of unity could be put. He would have made the new frontier coincident with the language frontier, and that line runs a few miles

METZ: THE GERMAN GATE.

To face page 192.

east of Metz. All the rest of Lorraine east of that line is German in speech, and so is the whole of Alsace. After one lifetime the welding would have been accomplished and the violent political partition forgotten. Unfortunately for the Hohenzollerns, the soldiers prevailed over the diplomat. A purely French town was included in the annexation, and it was this nucleus of anomaly which weakened the whole structure of German Alsace-Lorraine.

I know not how many morals may be drawn from that one incident, but the greatest of them is this : One man's work must be left to one man's brain and to one man's decision ; a single interference in his scheme may destroy the whole.

CHAPTER XXVII

TREVES

THE town whose native name is Trier, but which is called in English Treves, is yet again, like Aix-la-Chapelle, one of the essential historical points of Europe. It was the city in which the later Roman Emperors set up their thrones in order to stand against the frontiers and to watch the business of the barbarians.

Not that they, or anyone in the Roman Empire, regarded the barbarians as capable of destroying the Empire (nor did they destroy it); not that they or anybody else thought there would come barbarian conquests (nor did any such barbarian conquests come—they are the figment of the imaginations of dons, who, for some odd reason, love to exaggerate the barbarian), but because the Roman army, of which they were the chiefs and which was holding all Europe together, had become largely recruited from Slavs and Germans, and because other Germans and Slavs continually raided. The Emperors went to Treves because from Treves they could better watch the loyalty of federate troops under their command, who had brethren beyond the Rhine, and the barbarian raids which constantly threatened. Rome, be it remembered, was pushing outwards in influence much more than the barbarian was pushing in. The coasts from Calais up to the Elbe had learned to build boats after the Roman fashion, which made them formidable at sea, and already, under Julian the Apostate, the valley of the Main beyond the Rhine had plenty of good stone houses, built in the civilised fashion. It was this double movement, the influence of Rome beyond the Rhine, already apparent, and the German and Slav troops with the Roman army and the raids from those beyond, which made the later Emperors so often act from Treves and take Treves as their seat of government.

The era of this official greatness in Treves was not long ; perhaps a hundred years ; and even so, only intermittently during those hundred years. But it was long enough to impress the little town with imperial greatness, with the Roman grandeur. When a seat of government is thus planted in a place, even for short, interrupted periods, economic power of demand concentrates in the place and expresses itself in buildings—so it was with eighteenth-century Dublin, so it was with Santiago, in Galicia ; so it was with Avignon. Treves, holding the court now and again for short periods of the last Roman Emperors in the West, built great things with the money of that court. By a most happy accident, most of those great things remain.

For its size there is, perhaps, no place in Europe where the impression of our foundation, our roots in the old Græco-Roman society, is more evident to the eye. Not only does Treves preserve magnificent ruins, which are the finest Northern monuments of our Roman origins, but there is also about it an unbroken continuity. It has gone on from the Roman day to this, changing, but still itself. On each occasion, whenever I return to walk about its streets or to admire the very lovely statue, which was made only the other day out of limestone and is on the north-east pillar of the choir in Our Lady's Church, I feel, more than in any other town of Western Europe, more even than in little Pons, or in Pevensey (where also I feel it acutely), my lineage and your lineage.

The great evidence of the past in Treves, the stones of which all its citizens are most justly proud, the witness of antiquity, is the Black Gate, the *Porta Nigra*. It stands looking westward, down the Moselle valley, accepting the great route from Cologne and forming the most ancient entry into the city. Such evidences of the greatness of that ancient society once stood everywhere. Elsewhere, for the most part, they have been destroyed, save where the desert or some accident has preserved them. Timgad has

196

TREVES : PORTA NIGRA.

To face page 196.

its fine triumphal arch above the roadway;
Orange its entry under similar Roman masonry;
but Treves has something enormous and magnificent to show by way of a portal or introduction
to the town and by way of making us understand
what the town in the height of its glory must
have been.

The *Porta Nigra* was originally a great four-
storied building, ended and flanked by two big
bastions, the road entry into Treves from Cologne
and the Germanies passing through the round
arches in its centre, while, above this, barrack
rooms, or perhaps the quarters of civilian servants
took up the space.

It is astonishing how little it has lost in nearly
two thousand years, especially seeing that Treves
has been raided again and again, although I think,
not as badly sacked as have been other cities.
The south tower has been somewhat ruined, the
metal clamps of the stone have been robbed by
the soldiery of this, that and the other power,
notably, it is said, by the French in the revolu-
tionary wars; yet the structure remains, strong,
erect, imposing, not apparently changeable. It
impresses the mind much as an object of nature
may impress the mind, a mountain or an ancient
tree. I think if I had to show a man anywhere in
Europe some external, concrete, material thing
which would make him realise the nature of
our long past, and if I had only one thing to

197

show him, I would show him the *Porta Nigra* at Treves.

But Treves has much more to show. It is curious to note the Basilica which Constantine put up and which was, happily, I think, restored as a garrison church for the Prussian garrison before the war. I say 'happily' because this restoration has left us the building intact—there has been no destruction. Yet it is not a happy but an unhappy thing to see a place turned entirely from its old use and forming a kind of mixed body, half of the whole modern, half ancient. Not that the thing has been badly done —far from it—the proportions have been exactly observed; one side is old and the other side is new; but, in the new part, even the size of the Roman bricks has been copied accurately. It is quite a feather in the cap of the Prussian administration that this most ancient thing should have a modern use and should have been maintained alive. When I see its high arch of brick, I think of those ruined semi-domes in the Forum of Rome which also bear the name of the Basilica of Constantine.

Outside the city, to the south and east, lies the flattened ruin of the amphitheatre, yet there also, in spite of the decay of its ancient height, one feels the strength of the past, and I, for my part, many years ago, sat me down on one of the lower benches, which is covered now with earth, and

TREVES : OUR LADY'S CHURCH.

To face page 199.

pondered upon that arena ; wondering what the
sight was like when Constantine the Great, newly
arrived from York, threw to the lions scores upon
scores of Rhineland men who had attempted to
raid the Empire ; while, no doubt, their brother
Rhineland men, who had taken service in the
Roman armies, were watching, amused or im-
passive, under their Roman uniforms, the spectacle
of such a sacrifice. The garrison and the victims
were both Franks, but they felt no common bond.

Treves has, like all towns with any continuity,
a mass of the Dark Ages, of the Middle Ages and
of the modern centuries. Much more than
most towns, it suffers no jerk at any point between them. You may stand outside its ancient
cathedral and look curiously at the Roman stones
of its base, just as you may look curiously at them
at Aix-la-Chapelle. You may distinguish in the
structure the arches of the first Christian time, of
the later centuries of the Dark Ages, and you may
note, exactly adjoining, the new Gothic of the
Middle Ages in Our Lady's Church. Across one
of the streets an archway, bearing a stone crucifix,
powerfully reminds the onlooker of the religious
struggle following upon the reformation : quite
a modern thing. The fountains, the public
places, the remnants of the fortifications, everything in Treves is continuous : a series covering
two thousand years.

But of all its monuments I feel the old palace

of the Cæsars moſt. It is in complete ruin, it is
as ruined as the Roman wall of Silcheſter, or the
Thermes in Paris. Though its broken arches
ſtand high into the air, yet those halls are quite
empty, unroofed, a mass of weeds and grass and
trees, with the small Roman brick hanging together by its cement.

There it was that the great tragedy of Priscillian
was played out. That magician, around whom
such dark accusations lay, but who boaſted the
pride of a Chriſtian bishop in the beginnings of
the Chriſtian Empire, was dragged up here to be
tried. Here was he condemned; hence did he
go up to his death; and it was at the gates of this
mighty ſtruĉture, then in its glory, that one of the
greateſt of all our European race, Martin of Tours,
ſtood apart againſt the trial and conviĉtion—
insiſting that no matter what the man had done,
magician or no magician, he was a Chriſtian
bishop and could not be condemned by a lay
tribunal, even though that tribunal were imperial,
It is a marvellous ſtory, full of the change between the old pagan and lay conception of the
ſtate and the new theocracy. Here was it played
out, and these ruined brick arches of the Cæsars'
palace make me live it over again.

TREVES : A ROCOCO DOORWAY.

To face page 200.

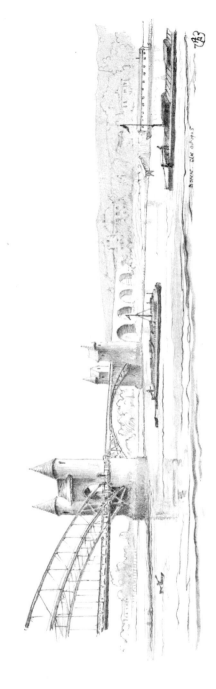

THE RHINE AT BONN.

To face page 201.

CHAPTER XXVIII

BONN

THE modern student of the Rhine, and all that the Rhine means for the future of Europe, will see in it, if he is wise, a great evil and a great interest The evil is the evil of modern industrialism ; the evil of the coalfields. The interest—an absorbing one—is the recovery of the Rhine as the chief highway of western Europe.

Nothing can now prevent the Rhine from being an international highway (and thereby a force making for European union) except some new unification of the German culture under some new conqueror, such as Prussia was in the lifetime before the Great War. If some such conqueror should appear, and once more create an exclusive German state, politically jealous, self-dependent, arrogant and including all populations of German culture, then it is conceivable that the Rhine should once again become a local, particular, national river, a cause of dissension and a threat to peace. But if, as is more probable, no such further conquest and welding into a new exclusive state appears, then the Rhine will remain what it now is—and promises to be still more in the future—a common bond for the material activities of Europe.

To-day that stream is an arresting sight for the eyes of a spectator who desires, as I do, a new and communal European life. You see upon its crowded water every flag of the states which reach its banks between the Alps and the sea, and even of those, such as Belgium, whose traffic comes to it by canals. You may see a French tug, towing a long train of very large, deeply-laden barges, and that train flying Dutch, Belgian, German colours. You will see a German tug performing the same office for another train in which the Swiss red cross and the French tricolour appear, and the whole of those hundreds of miles of rapid broad water remains in the mind like the memory of a crowded street. The Rhine has recovered the place which it held those hundreds of years ago when Christendom was united.

But all this has been made possible only by the presence of the great coalfield lying on its lower reaches, and by the industrial civilisation based upon that coalfield ; and it is here that you have the evil side of the thing. For no one will now deny that human happiness has severely suffered from the advent of these new powers. This disaster has not followed upon a mere material cause. It was not coal, or the mechanism which used it, that did us the harm : it was the rush of

ROLANDSBOGEN, ABOVE BONN.

To face page 202.

a sudden development with which we could not cope, and—much more—the false philosophy of avarice under which the development took place ; a greedy and individual error in the political action of man.

Take it all in all, the Germans have made a better job of the too-rapid expansion than we did. They had the advantage of coming much later. Our great towns sprawled out on coalfields, shapeless, hideous and morally anarchic. The modern German industrial system had greater opportunity to plan. None the less, here also the effect is evil. It is worst in the main towns of the Ruhr, it is bad in the great capital of the whole affair, Cologne, and all up-stream, wherever the great mass of transported coal is used for manufactory or has its effect upon other urban centres (such as Mayence), you have that deplorable degradation of life into a mechanical system, and of mankind into a disassociated dust of individuals, and of the works of man into the meaningless, or the disgusting or the absurd ; notably in architecture, and worst of all, in the architecture of the last twenty-five years.

But in the midst of this there remain the older towns and the far higher and older civilisation of the Rhineland. The contrast is almost as sharp as the contrast here in England between our cathedral towns and our sprawling manufacturing camps of brick and iron.

Of these older towns, the first upon which you come as you leave the coalfield going southward up-stream is Bonn. Its university, its typically Rhenish collegiate church, its traditional market-place, its unchanged streets, the noble line of its seventeenth-century park and of its stately academic buildings, all these are the older and the better Germany—which still survives, and which it may be an effect of the Great War to call back again into life under another form. Bonn has its roots in Rome. It stands where it does as a Roman frontier garrison upon the great river just below the Gorge.

This Gorge of the Rhine, that part of the river's course which has been so much more drawn and described, and known to our romantic fathers and grandmothers than all the rest of its course put together, is, geographically, a strange thing. It suggests the presence on the upper river of a great lake, the bed of which lay between the Swiss hills and the Taurus, and the flat bottom of which is now the Alsatian plain and the rich alluvial land to the north thereof. It is as though, in some cataclysm, a rift of sixty miles, sinuous and deep, had once cracked suddenly through the mass of high hills to the north of such a lake and drained it ; so that after the breach was made, the lake ran dry, leaving the upper Rhine winding through the midst of its emptied bed, the middle Rhine confined within that Gorge, the lower

204

RHINE : THE DRACONFELS.

To face page 204.

Rhine spreading out again through its flats to the North Sea.

This deep and narrow valley forms a short section of the whole story of the Rhine, quite separate from the rest in physical character and, therefore, in history. The crossings of the stream eastward and westward, for war or for commerce, lay below and above that Gorge. Roman Bonn watched the crossing below, Roman Mayence the crossing above : two gates. In that deep valley the confusion, the noise, the waste, and the despair of the great cities disappear. Every village, every ruined stronghold, maintains its position ; and to pass into it is like coming out from a factory into the countryside, or like reading a book of a better time, in which one may forget the surroundings of our own.

It is odd that these famous reaches of the great river, which had become almost ridiculous in the eyes of moderns for their theatrical setting and for the reiterated, somewhat clumsy legends which the guide-books emphasise, should now, in their contrast with what lies above and below them, have recovered so much dignity.

Who could have prophesied forty years ago that the over-picturesque rocks and ruins and rapids (the Lorelei, which had become a jest, and the Bishop's Tower, and the rest) would become classic under the pressure of new things and rouse our affections again ? Yet that is what they do to-day. I can imagine a man who had made his acquaintance with Ludwigshafen and Cologne swearing that he would never see the Rhine again unless it were above Bonn and below Mayence.

There is in all that piece of journeying up the Gorge nothing monstrous, unless it be the statue of William the First at Coblenz, on the cape between the Rhine and the Moselle; and that big and vulgar blunder is rather absurd than monstrous. But the great engineering works, notably the modern bridges of concrete or iron, which disfigure the river, are absent from the Gorge. You leave behind you one of the worst at Bonn; you are spared the sight of another until you are close upon Mayence.

In Bonn itself the note of antiquity is struck especially by the cloisters and their little, old squat palace, to which the Archbishops of Cologne were driven in the early Middle Ages when they fled from the rebellion of their capital city; and this typical monument of the German past is not a rare exception to be sought out in the midst of vilely different things (as are here and there such fragments in Cologne), but is native to the city and on a scale with it, as is the great church to which it is attached. The impression of antiquity here is strongly heightened by the massive simplicity of short pillar, rude capital (often unsculptured) and double rounded arch. It lacks the magnificence of that later work which

BONN : A CORNER OF THE DOUBLE CLOISTER.

To face page 206.

so weighs upon the mind at Worms and at
Spires, and which I shall next describe ; but it
the more suggests our passage from the Dark
into the Middle Ages, which transition such
small, very massive, domestic things recall. You
may see something of the same sort in the forgotten churches of the hills of Auvergne and in
the very oldest stones of the Jura. It is odd to
find it surviving here, and so thoroughly a part
of and a centre of a city right on the main river
of the Western World. It seems to belong
rather to the mountain regions from which travel
is diverted, and which have not the wealth to
rebuild. It is an introduction to all that tenacious
chain of antiquity which runs through the Rhine
Gorge above the City, and which, in ruin or in
careful preservation, or in mere survival, carries
on that soul of the Rhineland which an alien
Prussian rule from the east had so nearly ruined.

CHAPTER XXIX

WORMS AND SPIRES

WORMS and Spires are the two towns on the Rhine which a wise man would pick out as the two typical historic towns upon that river, because they share the historical interest of the rest of the Roman chain—Cologne, Coblenz, Mayence, Bonn, Basle—but, unlike all the others, have remained exactly themselves; Worms very largely, Spires entirely, has remained the city of the past, or, rather, has preserved its spiritual continuity.

Moreover, Worms and Spires are the two towns most intimately connected with that great turning point in the modern history of the West, the Reformation. It was at Worms that the new position was taken up definitely in the Diet there held. It was at Spires that the name ' Protestant ' took its rise, from the Protest of those in the meeting there held that they could not accept the decision of their ruler.

There is also about these two famous towns something which you will often discover in the intact relics of an earlier age ; and that is, the overwhelming proportion borne by the great church in the scale of the little city.

WORMS : OLD HOUSES ON MARKET PLACE.

To face page 208.

Elsewhere on the Rhine it is otherwise. Even the new mass of Cologne cathedral is lost in the modern industrial town which lives by the coal basin to the north of it. The ancient shrine of Mayence, with its doors of one thousand years, stands greatly in the midst of the modern industrial city, but is overwhelmed by that city.

In Worms and Spires it is very different. There the two majestic buildings, thundering (if one may use such a metaphor in architecture) with the last of the Dark Ages—two titanic structures in the round arch and the last expression of ancient strength before it was transformed by the vision of the French Gothic—occupy the eye from every side and challenge the sky.

What it is that gives this effect of mass in architecture no one can determine. It is, perhaps, a spirit in the builder, or, rather, in the mood of his time, surviving the centuries and still proceeding from that mind to ours. At any rate, so it is. You may show me modern buildings of which the actual measurements are superior in any degree to those of Worms and Spires, but not one of them produces the same effect of weight and enormity.

The two towns have this great advantage, as modern places go, that they are not on the main track of travel. Many expresses pass them; some few halt at Worms. Even Spires is reached easily enough. But they do not compel the traveller through the modern method of communication, and they are left fairly alone. It is a great advantage. For the traveller who would recapture the permanent spirit of the Rhineland it is an incalculable advantage—thus to be remote, spiritually at least, from the noise of modern Europe.

Of Worms the characteristic is rather the preservation of what was domestic and familiar among western Germans before the new industrial transformation. It is a town the old houses of which recall, as vividly as a well-acted play or a well-written historical novel, the German culture of the highest German time ; lovable, familiar, a little confused, but at ease and confident of itself. It is strange how fully that confidence can be felt in the spirit of the place, when one considers the passing and repassing of armies through it for centuries and the destruction wrought by the wars in that frontier-belt.

Spires more than Worms, indeed, more than any other little city I know in all the West, preserves itself wholly to itself.

I have written of Cherchell, on the Mediterranean coast of North Africa, and said, quite rightly, that it was a little paradise.

In quite another way, Spires has become an oasis of repose and quiet delight in my recent memories of travel. There is the same isolation,

Spires oct 1905 E.L.W.

SPIRES.

To face page 210.

the same silence, the same goodwill ; but the one is wholly of the North ; the other is of the burned and difficult Southern land held by arms. I could imagine a man with full liberty taking his ease for the proper months of the year alternately in Spires and in Cherchell.

At one end of the little town stands that high gateway, ' The Old Gate,' which is alive and august with the spirit of the German Middle Ages. At the other stands the great block of cathedral : spoiled, indeed, by a modern attempt at Gothic in its western end, but majestic in its multiple lines converging towards the sky throughout the rest of its structure, and provided with a measure of its vastness by the trees of the close or little park round about it.

Between the two runs the one great street of the place, very broad, quite quiet, at peace. There is not an electric tramway in the place. I had almost written (though that would be an exaggeration) that a man sauntering by those old doors from that most ancient shrine which was sacred to the Emperors, down to the tower height of the old gate, could even forget petrol and the stench and noise thereof. I cannot quite write that ; nothing in Europe to-day is free from the internal-combustion engine ; but, at any rate, Spires is as free as it is given to any modern town to be free of the modern evils ; and the people who inhabit it have for that reason retained a courtesy and a kindness which also the modern world has forgotten.

Spires is a place to return to, and I shall return to it, unless, as well may be, new troubles intervene. It is a city saved and content. Long may it so remain !

SPIRES : THE CATHEDRAL THROUGH THE TREES
OF THE CLOSE.

To face page 212.

CHAPTER XXX

THE VOSGES

IN one section only have the Marches something of a natural frontier; that section is the long line of rounded mountains spread with deep forest called the Vosges.

Very soon, I suppose, the Vosges will be well known. They will be visited by men of all nations, as to-day they are not, and as they have not been since railways first were laid down to their approach. Meanwhile, they still stand half apart, an attitude inherited from the abnormal fifty years, which only came to a close at the end of the Great War. From 1871 to 1919 an artificial frontier ran between the German conquests of the Franco-Prussian War and the territory of the French Republic. It followed the crest of these mountains; but that crest is not abrupt, and though it often (by no means everywhere) divides two forms of speech, it does not divide two races. These solemn, rounded hills, with their deep forests and leagues of solitude, their endless views to east and west over the Gauls and the Germanies, are altogether one thing; almost as much one in the soul of their people as in their

213

physical structure, which is nowhere interrupted by the precipice or the ravine.

I do not mean that the outer stamp of German architecture and manner on one side, French on the other, do not form a sharp contrast, for they do ; and that contrast is to-day accentuated by the political action of the last half-century. Put a man down in any one of the villages near the sources of the Moselle and he could not mistake a French village. Put him down in any village of the Munster or the Saverne valleys and he could not mistake an Alsatian one. But in the long formative centuries prior to the effects of central governments, in the great crucible of the Dark and Middle Ages and on, well into the seventeenth century, when countrysides formed naturally their own spirits and unities, the Vosges Mountains and their people were one thing, though cut by the boundaries of petty princedoms, of great dioceses and of monastic lands. The summer and the winter customs, the complex arrangement of water rights, forestry, pasture and the use of the streams were, and are, an inherited tradition throughout the range as much on the east as on the west side ; and were one thing until the mechanical barrier of 1871 was established.

During all the time covered by the lives and memories of those who to-day are not over sixty-five years of age, travel, growing universal throughout western Europe, has missed the unity of, and largely avoided, the Vosges. For during all that time this countryside, as large as a couple of English counties, was the seat of a latent war. On the one side were the packed garrisons of the French, on the other of the Germans. The line in between was closely watched by sentinels and police and spies, as a line is watched when hostilities may break out at any moment. Every obstacle was placed to travel back and forth. No new tunnel through the range was pierced from those early days of the Second Empire, when the main line to Strasbourg had built for it the tunnel of Saverne, to the present day. No great new road even, that I can call to mind, during all those fifty years of French road-building, was allowed to link up with the system beyond. The few passes served by such roads (the Schlucht, the Bonhomme, and so forth) remained with no addition to their number of any new passage for wheels. What had been left a footpath or bridle track between the pines when the Franco-Prussian War broke out, remained one throughout to the tragedy of 1914. Moreover, everything was done to prevent international as well as local travel across the range. At a time when all were free to go from one country to another without hindrance, this line was blocked by passports. The object of the government of Berlin was to compel travel to pass—and only necessary travel at that—by the two railways, neither of which really touches the mass of mountains.

Even the coming of the motor car hardly affected this hindrance. Every foreigner wandering on foot on the east side was suspect, as, indeed, were most natives; while upon the French side, the turning of all that district into one great camp hampered its use for any more human purpose. It is true that a good deal of tourist traffic developed locally, on either side of the range, especially on the French side. There were mountain stations for the summer and a growing knowledge of these hills; but the interruption of common travel from east to west as a whole paralysed the district; and the higher valleys, and the great sweep of woods, which form their unbroken character for many days of wandering, were almost unknown to Englishmen.

That will now soon change, with the evils and advantages following on such a change. I shall, for my part, regret the old loneliness, but no one can regret the restoration of natural freedom which will have broken that loneliness down. Before the war it was my custom, from the time when I was an undergraduate, to cross this frontier without formalities. I did so pretty well every year. There was a certain adventure about getting down from the forests of the escarpment on the side towards the Rhine, without running into the curiosity of questioning men; and in risking one's stay in the towns without a permit. It was especially amusing to watch the military manœuvres in the plains and to study discreetly the relations between the Alsatian people and the garrisons that kept them down with arms piled in the street; and their relations, also, with the new population which the German Government was steadily planting, especially in Strasbourg.

The sudden and great prosperity of Germany after the Franco-Prussian War, especially in the last half of the period, was nowhere felt more than in Alsace, and it was apparent that as time went on the work of transformation accelerated. There seemed to be here what you find throughout history, I think, and what historians so often neglect, that is, the effect of the unit of time formed by an average human life. Had the occupation continued for another generation, I believe that the old tradition would have been broken and that the crest of the Vosges would have come to separate two communities as sharply as an arm of the sea. As it is, the impress of those fifty years is still stamped upon the society of the Vosges. I saw it this year, in a singular experience in one of the higher eastern valleys, an experience you could not match in, say, the Cévennes (though there, also, two contrasting religions stand side by side), nor in the central Pyrenees, where you have two contrasting governments and languages.

Two villages stood upon either slope of a valley beneath the great forests which crown all the summits thereabouts. Between them ran a little mountain stream which had, I suppose, been the boundary of two lordships when the great religious quarrel settled down in the seventeenth century. The one of these villages, that one which was nearest to the crest, and, therefore, the nearest to the French-speaking people beyond, was Protestant. The other was Catholic. The separation in religion was sharper than you will get along the frontiers of the two religions in north-east Ireland, yet the relations between the two villages were familiar and intimate. The language of both was German ; in both French was spoken and understood ; in each it amused me to observe that the inscriptions upon tombs were German and in the Gothic script up to 1871, and after that in French and in the Latin script ; a very typical form of protest. Upon the Sunday the inhabitants of either village packed each its parish church, following each its separate rite ; and I noticed how the alien domination had not only preserved, but intensified, the religion of the Catholic village. At the High Mass everyone packed into the old building, the village *pompiers* stood in uniform along the central aisle in military fashion. Just before the elevation of the Host, three men filed out of the church armed and, as the bell rang, a salvo of guns was fired outside. That was something—the crowd of villagers, men, women and children; no one missing; the salvo of guns—which you would not have heard or seen in any other French province between the Rhine and the Atlantic.

It will be curious to note in what places the new travel of the Vosges will fix its centres. Munster, I think, will be one; Thann another. Gerardmer will remain, of course, another; but I can imagine that with the new opening of the roads, the northern half of the district will most lose its isolation. They will make more of Rothau and Ste. Marie and, perhaps, of St. Dié. What I profoundly hope will be spared—what I think will be spared—(which is the reason I do not hesitate to speak of it here) is that heavenly valley in the extreme south, which goes up into the heart of the ' Ballon d'Alsace,' and recalls to me the hidden higher valleys of California. Here the French army built a road (under long-distance and desultory fire) in the course of the Great War. Before 1917 there had been nothing but an ill-distinguishable path threading its way across high pastures and down through the very steep beech woods that overhang the lake below.

I say I do not think that this delightful garden of the Vosges will be overrun, because the new road will not tempt travel. The motors will, as is their providential habit, follow the main great way down to Belfort, or, if their destination is

Mulhouse, they will go by the Moselle valley and the Pass of Bussang. This diversion to the left will not serve their purpose, and I shall find it, I fancy, as much mine in ten years as I did not long ago, when I went down it with a companion, passing the emplacement of the battery by what is called the Black Rock, on the shoulder of the mountain, and looking down upon the lake and away towards the high side of the Black Forest, a day's journey off, beyond the Rhine.

Part VI
Tournai

CHAPTER XXXI

TOURNAI AND THE FIELD OF FONTENOY

THERE is an old town lying on the edges of the Teutonic-Flemish country northward of the French-speaking people and just within the modern boundaries of the modern State of Belgium. A sluggish river goes past its venerable quays ; its streets are inhabited by decent repose which only now and then a market or a fair disturbs. Its buildings have the dignity of the centuries ; grey houses of stone of the just proportions in which our fathers knew how to build. Its plan is of that irregularity which you find in all the undisturbed cities of Europe, and which grew up very slowly like an undergrowth of the original strict Roman parallels, right angles and squares. From far off its higher roofs stand against the sky in a fine outline and are framed in tall trees which dignify all that flat country land of Flanders. But in particular its ancient belfry shows against the grey sky of the north, and next against it five gaunt, enormous towers which mark the chief glory of the place, and, to me, the most interesting, I think, of all northern structures, the cathedral ; vastly more in scale than anything which a modern town of such a clime would erect; a sort of town of itself within a town; a spiritual keep, round which all the place gathers and up to which all its lines lead.

The name of this place is Tournai. It is forgotten; it is little more than a railway station to the chance travellers; it has achieved none of the fame which the later miracle of the Gothic has bestowed upon Amiens, upon Rheims, upon Rouen, upon Chartres, and twenty other towns. It might be thought hardly to count even in history, so little do men now remember it. The great industrial hive of Lille close by quite shoulders it out from the modern eye, for that is only a long day's march away, and those who pass it by have Brussels or Paris in their mind, or the Straits to which they are going and the crossing over to England.

It is well that it should be thus passed by and remain intact and unvulgarised in this time of ours when everything that is changed is changed for the worse. Thus it remains for the delight of such few as can take in the full pleasure of it and become one with its spirit; for the place is steeped in history and counts in a fashion more as a starting for the transition between Pagan and Christian times than any other of the North, while, centuries after that origin, it is the town of Fontenoy. Yet those who must concern themselves with the transition between the Roman

TOURNAI.

To face page 224.

society of antiquity and the Christian Europe which spread eastward thence, converted the Germanies, Hungary, the Poles, the Bohemians, Scandinavia, East England and built up what has since been Christendom, have forgotten Tournai and the Irish exiles, and do not hear the name of Fontenoy.

I have said that Tournai was the starting point of the great change from a Pagan to a Christian Gaul. It holds such a place in history for this reason : that it was the seat of government of the Merovingian kings. Here lies buried the father of Clovis, who here commanded the Roman garrison of the place, the King of the Franks, and here his tomb was found two hundred years ago, all Roman in design and spirit and the soldier within it Roman in his accoutrements.

When the universal society of the Empire had grown old and was losing vigour, when the seat of authority had been transferred to its distant Greek-speaking half and Constantinople had usurped the place of the Eternal City, the two great marks of the new time were the transformation of the army and the gradual establishment of the Catholic Church as the soul of civilised mankind.

The transformation of the army, very gradual, lasting over centuries, had changed it from an Italian to a provincial, and from a provincial to a half-barbaric thing.

Its recruitment had been drawn at first from the citizens of Rome alone, and by universal levy. That was in the very old times when the city was beginning its first steps towards universal rule and had gone no further than to extend a power over near neighbouring towns and tribes which were rather allies than subjects. That mastering army, as it vastly increased, still remained Italian in recruitment during the struggle with Semitic Carthage, which it destroyed, and during the sudden expansion over Gaul and Spain and the fierce civil wars between the great rival leaders of the Republic. Already in those civil wars there had appeared a certain foreign element; small bands of Germans hired by the competing generals had been seen in the field; certain Slavs, the Moors of the North African coast and Orientals too—it would seem here and there even some few Mongols. But the great bulk of the armed men were of Italian stock or Gallic. The great bulk of them had been born in the full tradition of civilisation and the army retained the character of that civilisation. But with the advent of the Empire, its peace, security and wealth, its vast extent, its preoccupation with frontiers against barbarism and the East, the nature of the Roman armies changed. Very gradually, imperceptibly, in a process which covers four hundred years, the legions grew sedentary, found their recruits from the men of the countryside wherein they were stationed, pensioned off their veterans with local land; continued the service with those veterans' sons. And, side by side with these, as the population now wholly civilian and increasingly averse to arms, gradually abandoned military force, there were enrolled ' federates,' as they were called, groups of half-civilised men from beyond the frontiers, barbarians, who desired nothing better than to enjoy the high civilisation which they interpenetrated but which they could not build. These bands, organised under their tribal chiefs as a rule, for the most part German in their origin and speech (though there were many other stocks among them, Mongol, Slav, Berber and the rest) come very gradually to be the main vital stock of the imperial forces. In the very end of ordered and united social rule, the two Roman generals who stood on Italian soil, now allied, now engaged in civil war one against the other—Stilicho and Alaric—were, the one a Vandal (that is, presumably a Slav with German admixture), the other a Goth. And all up and down the Empire you found, wherever you turned, garrisons and armies commanded by barbarians.

The change was fundamental, for Roman society was held together by the army and was governed as a military state. The word ' Emperor ' itself means nothing more than commander-in-chief; and title after title, to descend at last in much later times into other meanings, the duke, the count, the centurian, later the centenarius, were terms of military command and titles of military rank in the Roman service.

Before the end of the fifth century, between the years 400 and 500, just as the last powers of rule and taxation from Rome were ebbing away, when the Empire had ceased to renew the garrisons in Britain and later had ceased to send its officials into Gaul and Spain, government was taken over by the heads of these barbaric troops, Goth, Burgundian, Vandal and the rest. Nothing could have seemed more natural and more inevitable to the time. They were part of the Empire as they had always been, though that Empire had ceased to be a political unity. Its coins, its laws, the whole structure of its society, went on un-interrupted, but the executive power had passed to these local chiefs and, among them, one in the North particularly concerns us and Tournai.

He was the general in command of some small 'federal' force consisting in recruitment of 'Franks'—a term which does not stand for any particular stock or race, but for a confedera-tion, probably loose, and varying widely in size at different times, of armed bands along the lower Rhine and on the course of the Meuse and of the Scheldt. Such of them as lay beyond the Empire had often raided it and had suffered for their temerity, cut to pieces, thrown to the beasts of the arena, sold into slavery. Others had accepted Roman service as federates, and of these that group which was to be of most moment to the story of the world lay here round about Tournai, from which citadel the tribal chief or ' rex '—as the Romans called him—ruled. He was a Pagan and we know his name. His name was Childeric. He died and left a son, Clovis, no more than a lad in his sixteenth year, but accepted as leader and general through hereditary right. The general fought with another general of another band to the west of him, a certain Syragius, defeated him and joined the government of all that lay beyond the Somme to his own. It was from Tournai then that the great adventure started which was to lead to the final triumph of the Catholic Church.

For though Roman society was now in the mass Catholic, though there were now bishops in all the chief towns and the hierarchic organisation of the West was fully founded, yet by a curious historical accident, at first deplorable but destined to lead to the best of results, most of the local governments, their rulers and their courts, were Arian, that is, opponents and persecutors of the Catholic name, somewhat after the fashion in which the Irish garrison has been its opponent and persecutor.

These barbaric chiefs had got such a taint from the fact that the Emperor himself, his court and influence had been Arian at the moment when the

229

great change came. The new rising power in the far north, the army led by Clovis, the influence which had sprung from Tournai, was an exception. Its commander was Pagan. The few thousands of his command were a mixed body of Pagan Franks speaking the Flemish tongue, of Gallo-Romans and of ordinary citizens and barbarians. The ruler himself was not yet of the Faith.

In that he was married to a Catholic wife from the South, he was spared the hatred and animosity which the population and its leaders, the bishops, felt for the Arian rulers elsewhere in the West. While he was taking up the perpetual Roman task of driving out the barbaric raiders, the ceaseless Roman task of defending the Rhine frontier, he gained a victory at Tolbiac in the Rhineland (it would seem to be Zulpich) which he put down to the God of the Christians, upon whom he had called. On Christmas Day of the year 496 he was baptised with the Pagans of his little army, and from that moment there was a Catholic sword in Europe. The populace demanded Clovis. He marched south to their aid, he overthrew the Arian governments of the South, he began the reuniting of Gaul, and he died possessed of, and leaving to his sons, the enormous field of that quadrilateral between the Pyrenees and the Channel, the Atlantic and the Rhine, which was the heir of Rome, contained its living traditions and carried on its mission. He was still but a part of the Empire ; he thought it before his death a great honour to be given by the Emperor at Constantinople a subordinate title, but he was the sole true ruler of Gaul. It was from such a new foundation that the later universal rule of another house, the house of Charlemagne, was to spring, and it was from such a platform that the conversion and the subjugation and the gradual civilisation of all countries beyond the Rhine was to be made, until at last Christendom appeared in its fulness : Christendom which is to-day in peril.

And the point of origin of all this was Tournai.

It is no wonder that with such thoughts in mind a man approaches with awe, across the long cornlands of the plain, the five high towers, standing up towards the northern clouds. They mark, as I have said, the great church which rose upon the foundations of that earlier basilica wherein had been buried the founder of the French monarchy—of the ' men of the first race,' as the French call them (the second being the Carolingian, the third the Capetian).

It was not the Merovingian blood from Tournai which continued the line down through the centuries uninterrupted. The family decayed ; within three centuries another had supplanted it ; within three centuries again a third had taken over the rule of Gaul. But it was

the ruling family at Tournai which started the
tradition, which began the spread of the French
realm and from which the crown of France had
taken its rise.

Though there remains very little of that
original Roman church in which the Childeric
lay dead, clothed and armed for the tomb, yet
the cathedral at Tournai, rebuilt, carries on most
strongly its very ancient tradition of building.
The round arch is everywhere, the small low door,
the hugely thick wall, and, although it came so
many centuries later, a man looking from the
north, against the stern naked height of unre-
lieved stone which soars up in the growth of the
transept, is reminded of that Roman gate in
Treves. This impression of antiquity and of a
solid Roman thing is not destroyed by the later
apse, and though that apse has copied the pointed
arch of the Gothic, the general spirit of Tournai
still remains that of stones much older than the
spirit of the thirteenth century and conforms,
visibly stamped with limitation, the certitude, the
strength, of the Dark Ages. But there is even
very much later work within Tournai cathedral
which still does not detract from that weight of
a simpler past ; notably there has been flung
across the front of the choir a rood screen of the
Renaissance, exquisitely worked, and the side
chapels have altar glass, but though a man has
curiously noted each of these details in their

TOURNAI CATHEDRAL.

To face page 232.

excellence, there still remains with him as a permanent memory of the place those stark, exceedingly ancient walls, those small, round, weathered arches of lasting stone, those wholly simple short pillars which support them, and all the feeling of the time when Europe was standing at siege, yet hammering out against the North and the East the centuries before the great crusading march, the centuries of endurance and of perennial fortitude.

From four to three miles south-east of what were once the city ramparts, lies the famous battlefield of Fontenoy; the whole meaning of which turns again upon the town of Tournai, though under conditions wholly changed by the passage of so many centuries—1300 years since the place was the capital of Childeric's garrison and his little Roman army of Frankish soldiery.

Tournai was invested by the French armies in the great war of the Spanish Succession in 1745. There marched to its relief a large mixed force of English, Hanoverian and Dutch and a contingent of troops of Austria. They were met upon the rising ground east of the Scheldt. Louis XV., the King, was there with his heir, in the angle formed by the front of the defence which lay in right angle thrust forward against the attack, so that one side, to the right, was exposed to the Dutch advance; the other, that to the left and the north, to the English, Hanoverian and Austrian. Westward, beyond the river, high

batteries could just reach the enemy, and either
end of the French right angle reposed upon the
river.   At the apex of that front was the little
village of Fontenoy, which gives the battle its
name, but it should more justly be called ' the
Battle of Tournai ' ; for upon its issue depended
the fate of the siege of the campaign.   The
French strength in artillery was so great, their
defensive organisation was so strong, that it
seemed after the first attacks of that famous morning as though nothing could shake the line.   All
the first efforts against it broke down and that
with heavy loss when a final effort was made
by the English and Hanoverian troops.   It stands
out as the most vivid episode perhaps in all
European fighting between the Wars of Marl-
borough and those of the Revolution, and which
still, in particular, remain fixed in the tenacious
memory of the Irish because of the part they took
in the final stroke which decided the day.   The
English and Hanoverian column, very dense and
deep and dragging its few pieces with it by men's
labour, attempted the apparently impossible task
of forcing that defensive front after such heavy
and murderous failure during the preceding
hours.   The effect of their advance was profound
and unexpected.   Their discipline was so strong,
their fire so accurate and sustained, that they had
begun to throw their enemy into confusion
within the first half-hour of their advance.   The

battle, which had seemed already won for the French King, was imperilled, and might have been thought at one moment lost, so heavy were the casualties, so rapidly increasing the confusion in the line. There was a critical moment when it seemed indeed as though nothing could co-ordinate the spasmodic centres of resistance still remaining, but there entered into the action just at that decisive point the factor which Marshal Foch put tersely enough when he said that 'it was the last quarter of an hour.'

The attack all but succeeded, and it deserved to succeed, if only for the iron binding of the English and Hanoverian forces, and for that highest of the silent military virtues which it had displayed. Already the King of France had been warned to seek safety and had refused, and already the last efforts seemed upon the French side to be failing when Saxe, tortured as he was by the illness which killed him and only carried from place to place in his wicker chair at the cost of excessive pain, attempting to rally the dissipated and separate last forces of resistance, could see that the enemy advanced itself, the strict column which had not hitherto wavered and which had so penetrated as almost to dislocate his line, had not only reached but passed its breaking point of strain. It had all but conquered. It could not conquer because its bleeding and exhaustion was just in that turn of fate too much for it. Against

235

it, thus wavering, Saxe managed to rally and co-ordinate all that he had beneath his hand and to organise and to let loose a converging fire. The opposing column was on the point of breaking. Then did he launch the cavalry, and among them was that Irish brigade which has taken its place in legend. They were near the wood to the extreme left of the French line, and they covered the interval of fields at the trot, they charged on the now failing opponent with all the rest of the horse serving the King of France, and it was this cavalry charge which ended rather than decided the day.

The field lies to-day as do most of our European battlefields, deserted and silent. Its small woods are what they were so long ago—nearly two hundred years—its little villages are grown no larger. The sluggish narrow water of the Upper Scheldt crawls now as it did then up to the city northward and through its quiet quays; and from the highest points to the stage upon which all that carnage was played out, one sees against the northern sky much what one would have seen so long ago, specially those five giant towers of the cathedral. You find upon Fontenoy, as you find upon the land of Waterloo, of Crécy, of Blenheim and of nearly all the great battles, a peculiar and haunting silence and a vivid absence of men which makes the memory of the place the more inhabited by the past.

Nearly all the great battlefields affect me thus, none more than this open, windy place under the Flemish sky, with the shafts of the cathedral to the north and the quiet of Flanders all around.

Part VII
Three Towns of Life and Death

CHAPTER XXXII

NARBONNE

UPON a Whitsunday I found myself returning from the Balearics, through Spain, to that luxuriant warm plain between the mountains and the sea, which the Romans knew as the "Narbonnese." It was the wealthiest diſtriꜩ of their Gaul; grouped round its great central port; the pole of so much energy, superb achievement and tradition.

I had spent these spring weeks, from April onward, in passing through the recovered countries of Sicily, North Africa and Spain, drawing and writing upon the towns in which our civilisation has re-established itself, so gradually, recovering them from the flood of Mohammedanism in which they had been for centuries drowned.

Here, in the Narbonnese, I was at the end of that excursion and back again in the unbroken tradition of our people and of the Faith. For though the Saracen flood had indeed beaten upon the walls of this place, and though sundry small garrisons of Islam had lingered on between the Pyrenees and the central mountains of France, yet they had not here occupied, ruined or transformed, as they occupied, ruined and transformed elsewhere. And Narbonne catches on back through 2000 years to its origin without interruption, and has, stored up within itself, the very essence of Rome. It was in these fields that the great landed family, the highest name in whose lineage was that of Charlemagne, had its origin and root.

For Charlemagne was, on his father's side and by direct descent, the head of the Ferreoli, Roman nobles of the Narbonnese.

The place is better suited for the conservation of the past and for the handing on of most ancient memories to us, the modern passers-by, from the fact that it is decayed. Those great centres of Europe which have been continuously active from the Pagan days to our own, have largely destroyed, with rebuilding and with the change of fashion, the material objects of their inheritance. But towns which have been arrested at some moment and fossilised, as it were, present the remote past, and we can live it again within their walls.

It is so with Narbonne. The great port which had been filled for so many centuries with all the shipping of the Mediterranean, which had been greater than Marseilles or Genoa, had rivalled Naples opposite, and was the queen of all that coast between Tarragona and the Atione, slowly filled. The land rose in one of those imper-

242

ceptible movements which change political geography, and the great land-locked bay turned, as
the centuries proceeded, into a shallow lagoon,
with but one issue, where a small port called the
New Port continued to carry on perhaps one-
hundredth of the trade that the mother city had
once conducted. That mother city slowly turned
to a shrunken, inland place, its ancient function
lost.

And the date of the turning point, when at
last the narrows had become too difficult, and the
harbour too shoal for a continued life, is well
fixed by the enormous cathedral and palace of the
Bishop, which stand like a fortress, and are yet
uncompleted, halted at mid-building in the very
midst of the Middle Ages.

The Palace of the Popes at Avignon, nearly
contemporary, is larger and even more solid in
effect, but it does not pretend to combine church
and stronghold. Here in Narbonne both the
ideas are commingled and form one thing. Coming upon it from the outer streets, if you approach
by the palace side, you see indeed the buttresses
and the ogives of a Gothic church, but there is a
strength and bigness, a massiveness of stone, a
reduction of ornament, which still suggests the
fortress and the keep.

Next you notice that the huge thing is incom-
plete. It was never finished. It has an apse
with transepts only begun, and where the nave

should be are only the unconnected juttings of great stones squared for the builder and uncontinued.

But this effect of power and of resistance, this character of standing for a siege, which is the chief mark of the cathedral of Narbonne, disappears in a sort of magic and a transformation when one passes the door and gets within. Then all is suddenly changed into a place of coloured light. And that which externally was all shoulders and masonry, seeming to allow but small open spaces between, from within is one great round of those solemn and soaring windows which turn the greater glories of the thirteenth century into a vision.

When I thus came to Narbonne, it being yet long before noon in the mid-morning, a strong May sun poured through that glass and made the whole airy cavern celestially alive. It seemed to have (though it had not actually the measurement) the height of Beauvais, the majesty of Paris, and something of the magic of Chartres.

For the thirteenth century learned to work this miracle of contrasts : so to arrange the external stonework that its characteristics to the onlooker from without was the strength of this world, but so to devise the interior with the least proportion of fine, long-drawn supports, that the lights were its universal mark, and that the building itself seemed half air.

I came to the town juſt in time for the Great High Mass of Pentecoſt, and going ſtraight to the palace and paſt it into the cathedral, I took my place in what were once the ſtalls of the canons (for, as I have said, there is no nave, and only the choir is roofed), till the procession entered, and the Sacrifice began.

It was an experience such as I shall not have again, I suppose, in this life; such as I had not had before in all the many years and towns of my travels. For there met in combination there, by some divine chance, certain ſtreams of emotion, their combination all enhanced by the quality of the place. What I had just seen in Barbary, the several crossings of the Mediterranean Sea, the town under the ſtrong light, the mountains to the south and to the north, far away, the richness of the plain, the great ſtory of aƈtivity and of decay, all this combined to give an immense significance to this which I was about to follow, this Aƈt, repeated daily upon ten thousand altars, which is also more significant than anything else in the world.

It was as though this High Mass which was about to open had something about it especial; catching up the spirit of the myriad others which in succession were rising to meet the sun in the progress of morning light around the world; and I was filled with the recolleƈtion that I had chanced, by the beſt of fortunes, to find myself here upon the Feast of the Holy Ghost. It was a little after nine o'clock of the morning of that Whitsunday.

Men are often blamed (and more often justly blamed) for permitting the sensual to invade the intellectual ; that is, for allowing their judgment (which is our highest faculty, after love) to be warped by the appetitive in man.

On this account it is that the detestable Manicheans (for whom the modern name is ' Puritans ') reject the proper glories of public worship and the unison of the whole of man into the act of God's praise and of God's service. Without considering their unhappy malformation, it remains true that a man must never misinterpret his mere emotion for faith, nor his mere mood for intellectual assent and conviction ; still less must he ever substitute intention for act, and a feeling, however strong, for achievement. Faith is of the will. He would be a poor heir of the Catholic Church who would consider the splendours of her most noble pageantry in the greatest Mass, as in some way adding to the inward values and to the unseen glory of a low Mass said hurriedly in some chapel of a hamlet.

Nevertheless, I would advance it to be true that the soul is supported by all sacramental things ; that is, by all unison of the mind and the body upon a proper object ; and that when great architecture and glorious colour and solemn music, and the profound rhythms of the Latin tongue, and the ritual of many centuries, and the uncommunicable atmosphere of age, all combine to exalt a man in his worship, he is made greater and not less. He is supported. He is fed.

Well do I know that the greatest of visions have come to men in small rough huts of stone, round in shape, piled by their own hands above the Western seas of Ireland or in the Hebrides. And I know very well that these men scaled heaven.

I know also that men similarly isolated in the deserts between the Nile and the Red Sea perceived our final inheritance and were admitted into divine company.

There is no necessity of any aid from the senses; and the greatest of those who were adepts in the search for heaven did, upon the contrary, withdraw themselves from all influence of the senses when they most desired the satisfaction of the *prægustatum*—the foretaste of that for which we were designed : our home.

But I cannot boast myself to be of such a kind, and on my own poor level it is landscape, the sea, human love, music, and the rest, that help to make me understand : and in their absence I am very empty indeed.

Now here in the cathedral of Narbonne, upon the Whitsunday of 1925, having so come in with one companion in the morning of a hot summer's day, after so much exploration of the heights of Africa, so much watching of the conflict between Islam and ourselves, so much content in the glories of Spain and in the peace and wealth and good manners of Palma, of Majorca, so much breathing of the Mediterranean air in long nights upon the decks at sea, certainly all the support requisite, all the augmentations valuable to a man of my kind, came very fortunately together ; and I received, at this Whitsunday High Mass in the cathedral of Narbonne, what I had desired to receive : a great good.

The over-cautious heretics who misunderstand the end of dignity do not confess these things to their fellow beings.   But I am willing to confess them, well knowing, first, that dignity is of another kind ; secondly, that whatever has done oneself good should be communicated to others ; and, thirdly, that the whole affair lasts only for a little time, and that we are bound upon a very different journey from that of this world.

Well then, the Mass began.   They bore above the head of the celebrant priest that round shade of silk which had also come centuries and centuries ago from Rome.   They had their particular rites of the bishopric, and of their tradition. They read the Gospel, not from the altar steps, but from high up near the roof, above the heads of the whole people ; from the organ loft, in splendid fashion.   And when they sang the *Veni*

Creator, I could swear that the spring sunlight which fell coloured on the stone floors took on another quality.

And I remembered the singing of that same song on the great day when St. Dominic sang it upon the scaling ladder, and our people stormed the wall and destroyed the mortal Albigensian peril, and restored Europe.

I must tell you that all this time the Blessed Sacrament was exposed above the altar on a very high place in a blaze of light. The Mass proceeded; the final prayers were said; the thing was over.

If I could have got into that nave of Narbonne all the starved, unbelieving men cut off from the past in the dissolution of our modern world, there would have come out some reasonable proportion restored to the traditions of Europe.

CHAPTER XXXIII

CHAISE DIEU

O N the level summit of a mountain-land, not isolated, yet above the general confusion of the bare hills—looking over a deep toward the sombre wall of the Margeride beyond —stands the Chaise Dieu. It is a church of granite, enormous, forsaken and alone. Attached to it, a sort of fortress, hangs a cube of high-walled building, equally huge and deserted, which once held its community. A sombre warden keep or tower and a guarded gate, deep like a tunnel, watch toward the east. The face of the great shrine watches toward the west; but it seems blind or fixed, without that movement in stone, that expectation, which is the note of Christian shrines; without that serenity which is the note of Pagan. It is enchanted; not asleep, but gazing dumbly; and its sheer blanks of wall confront time. They are very dark; and their simplicity is more than austere, for it has about it something of doom. The two square towers which our civilisation sets upon the face of its temples are here the two strong limbs of a giant beast, neither in repose nor at bay, but eternally awaiting. I know nothing like it in Europe.

About the great affair still gathers a little town, impoverished since the life of its overwhelming maker sank into such silence. The inns are small and ill-frequented. The flow of human power has left the hill and its wealth is no longer gathered. I believe that few to-day have seen or know the place or even read of it. Yet one of the main roads to the south passes over that summit. Le Puy, which all the world talks about, is a day's walk upon one side; Vichy—which might be Ascot or Nice—is two days' walk upon the other. The Chaise Dieu is preserved by that ironic power which sends wealth to live down noisy highways and protects whatever desires to be silent and to endure. It can build up its memories within itself and await securely the return of its business. No sound disturbs it.

The name it bears signifies ' The House of God '—' Casa Dei' (for the mountaineers of Central France soften the Latin ' c ' into ' ch ') —and that name hangs fittingly about the mighty roof; it is consonant with the purpose of those stones : their centuries of strength, their un-changeable hard lines, their purpose of resur-rection. If ever too great a title might be excused it is here. For there is a sense both of habitation brooding about the stronghold and of supre-

macy ; and each of these its soundlessness to-day
enforces.

Its foundation was new when they fought at
Battle ; the later stones are of the fourteenth
century. It will not seem older in a thousand
years. The profound and simple windows which
pierce its man-deep sides might be unglazed and
a passage for storm-winds without affecting its
aspect. Its monstrous oak doors might be taken
away and yet leave the aspect the same. It
depends upon no ornament ; but is a majesty in
itself, in its proportion and assize, its weight
upon the rock from which it was hewn. The
hurricanes of winter on these Avernian summits,
their long depths of snow, and their frosts so
near the stars, and the brazen heat of their
summers on the bare uplands, do nothing to the
exact fitting of those stones or to their surface ;
less than to the quarries whence they came. It
is as though the men who built them up and
squared them had known spells ; or as though
they had been given power to bridge across decay
from their own time, through ours, to a return.

I came upon all this through the deep woods
which cover the mountain on its northern slopes
and cease towards its summit. I discovered the
mass of the thing suddenly, not a mile off, towards
the approach of night. Indeed the evening was
far advanced, the trees had already grown dark
against the smouldering sky, and the water of the

ponds had taken on that dead flat white which
they present to the beginning of darkness, when
I came upon those harder lines of granite and that
black immensity towering. I entered by a very
broad and high archway to the side of the church
in the monastery wall. I went up a flight of steps
made as though for a host of men, as broad as a
river, dark now, and echoing too loudly to a
single tread; there was no voice near: nor any
other sound. I came abruptly into the awful
emptiness of that nave. The last glimmer of
light, within, barely distinguished floor from wall,
and the roof was all gloom. The powerful arches
of the windows were exactly cut against the last
faint colour from the west. I stood there till this
had wholly faded, and the first stars were seen.

With the morning I returned. The solemnity
of the place was oddly greater under the effect of
day. And this was because the bare stones, upon
which in the darkness one might have imagined
relief, were seen to be unadorned. The effect was
greatly emphasised by the one monument the
place contained.

For, in the midst of the church, stands an
exquisite tomb, the tomb of that Avignon Pope,
Clement, who had concentrated so much wealth
upon this rebuilding of the Chaise Dieu, and who
desired to connect it for ever with his name. The
tomb is of black and white marble, and the
anarchists of the Huguenot rebellions (who went

about destroying all they could of ancient beauty) shattered the minor statues wherewith it was surrounded. I am not sure that they did not increase the value, through isolation, of what remains : the noble figure of the dead, and the contrasting simplicity of the twin-coloured stone. There is a Dance of Death upon part of the wall ; there are also tapestries hung, not very large. There is woodwork, but not of a sort enriching or dominating the great space, and, for the rest, there is still this strange emptiness, as though the whole place were a tomb, with this one reclining figure in its midst.

Even if one had not heard a word of the long history one would know the place to be haunted. Here Anselm waited upon the mountain height for the message from Rufus. That is truth— but there is also an odd legend. For men here showed the tomb of Edith, the Confessor's Queen, Harold's sister. Yet surely the Conqueror had her buried by her husband's side at Westminster ? I know not how the story arose, but they seemed convinced that she came in her widowhood to retirement here and here died. She was the only one of Godwin's hateful blood for whom men could find a good word. But how came she to be linked with this deserted hill ?

That, then, is the Chaise Dieu. I left it by noon to go down the long mountain slope to-

wards Le Puy. To my right, as I journeyed, still
stood endless, level and high, the blue ridge of
the Margeride; and I could fancy to hear—
though it was a long day's walking away—the
tumbling of the torrent Red Cap, which roars
through its gorges. Before me and to the left,
the Cévennes showed an indigo edge of lump and
peak. All about me was the burned land. But
the landscape was filled with the spirit of the
Chaise Dieu as a garden is changed and informed
by music.

I could wish to return in a hundred or two
hundred years and see whether my guess that the
great place should come into use again had proved
true or false; for certainly it bears the air of a
foundation intended to endure, and to be restored
to life.

CHAPTER XXXIV

CORNETO OF THE TARQUINS

CORNETO ſtands upon a rocky hill that overlooks the Mediterranean, three miles away
and below, over a dead-flat plain of marsh
and fever.   It is the town of the Tarquins.   Its
name is ſtill ' The Tarquinian.'   Its gate is the
Tarquinian Gate.   That great lordship ſtill hangs
over Corneto ;   the family that gave Kings to
Rome.   They might return after twenty-five
centuries and find the place ſtill their own ;   for
it is ſtill Etruscan, and, what is more, Etruria has
here risen from the dead.   The thousand tombs
have sent back to the light ſtrong faces in ſtone,
and ſtone coffins sculptured with the fates of the
soul, and vases carrying every piĉture of that life,
and the ornaments of women—still to be worn.
The spirits have refused to leave that ground.

It was the sacred and perhaps the chief of the
Etruscan cities—the one lying moſt to seaward,
and that which had outside its wall a national
cemetery ſtretching for miles to the eaſt and the
south.   Above the sharp precipice to the landward, where the wall ſtands moſt forbidding and
with its moſt ancient foundations apparent, a man

sees from the ramparts that cluster of mountains, the old volcanoes, which are the makers of an undying race ; the burnt land of Tuscany, mother of Gods and Kings. None knows whence the blood came, or sprung from the very earth or brought in from over-sea ; but that same soil where the old fire smoulders underground and where the silent craters hold very wide lakes of water high above the world in their rims, that same igneous dust which subtly strengthens the vine, made the Etrurian people and through them the iron laws, the subterranean vision of death, the dusk of religion, which they imposed on Rome and from which we all inherit.

For, indeed, the business of the soul and the doom of man haunted this people. On the day when I watched the mountains to the east from the walls of the Tarquinian crags—mountains of Orvieto, of Volterra, of all the federation—angry storms swept those summits, and the Sirocco piled clouds above the heights and veiled them here and there with rain ; though westward, towards the sea, it was already clear. It was under such storms a man could best brood over the sweep of slope and barren rising down, which hid (save for small entries of white against the dark wrack) the miles of tombs.

I did not descend among them, among those dead. I did no more than walk out through the early evening into their vast, deserted field. I came back before the end of the day to look at the great stone coffins which have been gathered in the museum of the town.

Though that museum is a lovely palace of the later Middle Ages, I found no shock of discontinuity between the time of the tombs thousands of years ago, of the palace five centuries ago and my own time in the quiet town. All had grown ; and, what was more, the domination of the founders has so impressed itself upon Corneto that the oldest things and the latest are in the same air.

With what majesty are the stone faces upon those very ancient coffins hewn ! I saw one there of a young man not awakened, as it were, from sleep, but upon the point of waking ; the face turned to the left in a complete repose which had yet about it something stern ; half the head was lost in the material, left rough, from which the whole was carved, suggesting those modern tricks which Rodin affected and vulgarised. Here, in this immemorial thing, there was no suggestion of trick or effort. Some instinct, not a willed effort, prompted the man who chiselled it to leave uncarven the body of stone upon which the profile reposed. On the sides of the coffin beneath were sculptured those dreadful figures which in the dark origins of religion (or, more probably, the dark inheritance of some fall and failure from a better creed) peopled the places below the earth.

It would seem that this ancient nation thought

of the soul in its passage as something hunted ;
yet there was here no note of terror—which is
always unworthy of art, a weakness and a defile-
ment—but there was certainly a note of darkness
and of peril. More, still, was there a certitude
of immortality. For though it be true, as it is
true, that the full doctrine of immortality which
has made Europe the head of the world, came to
us ultimately from the islands of the Atlantic Sea ;
though it be true, as it is true, that the last edges of
the West, the great salt cliffs of Ireland, of Brittany
and of the Hebrides, are first found possessed of
that revelation and sent it in a distorted message
through Britain and Gaul, till at last it awakened
even Syria ; yet here in these Etruscan tombs, as
in the Egyptian, the quality of immortality was
apparent ; an adumbration or a memory : confused, I think ; perhaps without dogma, and
therefore unrooted ; but certainly there.

This marriage of living and of dying, this
obsession with the passing of the soul, was
apparent again in the superb figure of a matron,
upon whose tomb the sculptor had revived what
was surely her very body ; for never have I seen
any stone living more intensely with personality.

There was little or no action. It was a head
raised, and the shoulders with it slightly ; the
movement of a strong frame attending to some
speech, but still reclining and fully in repose.
There was no pretence to beauty, not even to a

beauty lost, in that face of middle age, but a singular majesty and a full bearing of that burden which we, the Christians, in our later age, call also the duty of living. Of what sons was she the mother? Of what soldier the widow, or of what lord? What fields were the fortune of the great family from whom she inherited? What slaves of what household thronged her funerals?

If ever there was a face made for ever, it is that face! I shall come back to it again. For Corneto, once seen, is a place to which a man returns as he returns to the Capitol or to his home. Corneto, once seen, inhabits the mind and becomes an habitation for the mind. For there you have the impress, memorial and perpetuation of a great people, wholly preoccupied with the great business not only of life, but of death.

Were I to add also something on the strength of that dead mother's face, I might mislead my readers; for clearly this people were not concerned with strength save as a means to an end. Nor did the artist know, I think, when he made that superb head and fixed its life and its death for eternity (or so much eternity as there is in even the hardest stone) that he would give to one coming so long after any message of strength. He was concerned rather with a purpose fulfilled and with the dignity and completion of the woman whom he thus established. Therein might be seen all the affair: the bearing of children; the governance of a household : the loss of this and that affection and companionship ; and all, whatever losses beside, make up the burden of mankind. Therein also was the last descent out of the light of the sun ; the loss of the light of the sun ; the last and mortal loss of all. The weight of a lifetime, so borne, was in that face, and a resolute acceptance of the end.

When I had left my long contemplation of that face, I went up upon the ramparts of the city and looked out over the sea. The hills run down abruptly, lovely enough. The flat between it and the surf line has nothing of our northern seasides, nothing enjoyable or livable, but rather is it a barrier where men do not live. Also the sea, empty of sails at the ending of that day, enhanced the effect of desertion and silence. The sun was sinking unclouded into the even line of the Mediterranean. The storm clouds had gathered up far to the east in a mass of gloom upon the mountains. All was the symbol of life ending and darkness beyond.

Then I thought to myself, as I so looked westward from the wall, how men might say of the life of all our race as of the life of one, that we know not whence it came, nor whither it goes.

For there is no introduction to Corneto. These great dead, their powerful art, their living, immortal stones, spring out from a remote beginning, with no hint of what power formed them ;

nor did they themselves pretend to tell us, nor, I think, did they themselves pretend to know what origin there might be for so much, so greatly made ; their walls, their ritual, their tombs, their effigies !

This place, how many thousands pass in a week along the main line that runs below Corneto from the north : from Leghorn, from Genoa, from the slime of the Riviera, from Paris, from London, all on their way to the hotels of Rome. And how many know what they are passing ?

They are passing the things of life and of death.

THE END.

PRINTED IN GREAT BRITAIN BY ROBERT MACLEHOSE AND CO. LTD.
THE UNIVERSITY PRESS, GLASGOW.